The Horten Ho IX/
Ho 229

(including the Gotha Go 229)

Airframe Detail No.8
The Horten Ho IX/Ho 229
(including the Gotha Go 229)

– A Technical Guide
by Richard A. Franks

First published in 2020 by
Valiant Wings Publishing Ltd
8 West Grove, Bedford, Mk 40 4BT, UK
+44 (0)1234 273434
valiant-wings@btconnect.co.uk
www.valiant-wings.co.uk

© Richard A. Franks 2020
© Richard J. Caruana – Colour Profiles

The right of Richard A. Franks to be identified as the author of this work has been asserted in accordance with sections 77 and 78 of the Copyright Designs and Patents Act, 1988.

The 'Airframe Detail' brand, along with the concept of the series, are the copyright of Richard A. Franks as defined by the Copyright Designs and Patents Act, 1988 and are used by Valiant Wings Publishing Ltd by agreement with the copyright holder.

All rights reserved. No part of this publication may be reproduced or transmitted in any form or by any means, electronic or mechanical, including photocopy, recording, or any other information storage and retrieval system, without permission in writing from the publishers.

Please note, whilst we are always happy to hear from readers, we are not in a position to enter into discussion (in person, in writing or via electronic mail) with any individual, nor to undertake or supply research/supporting material relating to this, or any of our other titles. Our apologies for this, but it is inevitable if we are to meet our production schedule each year and all sources (excluding those from private collections) are listed in the bibliography.

ISBN 978-1-912932-10-8

The Ho IX V1 outside the garage in which it was built being towed to the nearby airfield for final assembly

Sections

Introduction	5
1. Technical Description Detailed coverage of construction and equipment	17
2. Camouflage & Markings Colour side profiles, notes and photographs	48
3. Small Scale Horten A build of the 1/72nd scale Ho 229 kit from the recent combined 1/144th and 1/72nd set from Zoukei-Mura by Libor Jekl	57
Appendices i Ho IX/Ho 229 Kits ii Ho IX/Ho 229 Accessory & Mask List iii Bibliography	64

Note regarding images etc.

In creating this title we have sourced as many photos that exist of the type, however with only a limited number of airframes in total there is little in the way of official images and when you combine this with the fact that the type was never officially adopted by the Luftwaffe this means there is no flight manual nor parts list. As a result, we have used the best images we can find, but inevitably at times the quality of some of this material is not as good as we would have liked.

Note

There is much debate and some confusion with regard to the designations of Horten designs, many current aviation authors state that only the letter 'H' prefixed the type (e.g. H VII), however during WWII all Nazi German aircraft manufacturers used the first two characters of their name to precede the RLM type number (e.g. He for Heinkel, Ju for Junkers etc.). However the first system, to me, just looks wrong in print and for consistency with other aircraft types mentioned in the narrative we have adopted the term 'Ho' to precede any Horten type number. Also note that the Horten brothers used Roman characters (e.g. Ho II, IV, IX etc) for the type instead of Arabic (e.g. Ho 1, Ho 4, Ho 9 etc.), although you will come across both in post-war evaluation documents and many written accounts since. Finally many of you will have seen the term 'Go 229' being applied to the type in relation to the V3 and projected production, however in reality the type would have been the 'Ho 229' once it reached production, regardless of the fact that such production would have been sub-contracted to Gotha. We have therefore opted to use Roman numerals for the early designs (including the Ho IX) and Ho 229 in all references to the V3 onwards throughout this title. There are also many different ways of writing Luftwaffe aircraft designation, however for consistency we have used one style, e.g. Ho IX V1, Ho 229 V3, Ho 229A-1 etc.

The Ho IX V1 flares out on landing at Göttingen in the summer of 1944 - note the water sprinklers in the background

Glossary

BMW ....Bayerische Motorenwerke (Bavarian Motor Works)

DB ....Daimler-Benz

Erprobungskommando ....Test Detachment

Erprobungsstelle (E-Stelle) ..Test Centre

ETC ....*Elektrische Trägervorrichtung für cylinder bomben* (Electrically operated carriers for cylindrical bombs)

Feldwebel (*Fw.*) ....Sergeant (RAF) or Airman 1st Class (USAAF)

Flieger ....Airman

Funkgerät (*FuG*)...................Radio or Radar Set

Fw ....Focke-Wulf Flugzeubau GmbH

General..............................Air Marshall (RAF) or Lieutenant General (USAAF)

Generalleutnant....................Air Vice-Marshall (RAF) or Major General (USAAF)

Generalmajor ....Air Commodore (RAF) or Brigadier General (USAAF)

Geschwader..........................Fighter Wing comprising three *Gruppen* and one *Stab*

Gruppe ....Group

Hauptmann (*Hptm.*) ....Flight Lieutenant (RAF) or Captain (USAAF)

Jäger..................................Fighter

Jagdgeschwader (JG) ....Fighter Wing

Jumo...................................Junkers Motorenbau

Kommando...........................Detachment

Luftflotte..............................Air Fleet

Major..................................Squadron Leader (RAF) or Major (USAAF)

MG....................................Machine Gun

Oberfeldwebel (*Ofw.*) ....Flight Sergeant (RAF) or Master Sergeant (USAAF)

Oberleutnant (*Oblt.*) ....Flying Officer (RAF) or Lieutenant (USAAF)

Oberst ....Group Captain (RAF) or Colonel (USAAF)

Oberstleutnant (*Obstlt.*) ......Wing Commander (RAF) or Lieutenant Colonel (USAAF)

OKL....................................(*Oberkommando der Luftwaffe*) Luftwaffe High Command

Reichsluftfahrtministerium..(RLM) Reich Ministry of Aviation

Revi (*Reflexvisier*) ....Reflector Gunsight

SC..*Sprengbombe Cylindrisch* (Bursting Bomb*, Cylindrical)

SD ....*Sprengbombe Dickwandig* (Bursting Bomb*, Thick-walled)

Staffel...................................Equal to Squadron in RAF

Stammkenzeichen.................Primary identification (code letters)

Technisches Amt ....Technical Department of the RLM

Unteroffizier..........................Corporal (RAF & USAAF)

Versuchs or *Versuchsmuster*.Research or test aircraft (V-series)

Werknummer (W/Nr.) ....Works (construction) number

* – Fragmentation bomb

Cutaway drawing by Richard Keller at Horten of the original BMW 003 powered Ho IX with 16m span

A rear view of the Ho IX V1 being towed out to take-off at Göttingen

The Horten Ho IX V1 nearing completion after being converted from its original intended powered version to an unpowered sailplane

Introduction

Brief History

The Treaty of Versailles prohibited powered flight in Germany in the interwar period, so many young Germans learnt to fly with gliders at the Wasserkuppe, situated about 100km from Frankfurt. Amongst them were the Horten brothers, Walter, Reimar and Wolfram and it was Reimar and Walter who

won the scale model flying competition there three years in a row (1931, 1932 and 1933) with their own flying wing glider designs. Walter entered military service in 1934 and transferred to the new Luftwaffe in 1935, whilst his two brothers were called up into military service in 1936. Walter became a

The Horten Ho IX V1 outside the garage in which it was built prior to movement to Göttingen airfield for final assembly. The open box in the rear is for the braking parachute

A nice comparison, the earlier Horten IIIe design sits behind the Ho IX V1 outside the Junkers hangar at Göttingen

fighter pilot and saw action in the Battle of Britain with JG26 and test flew a captured Supermarine Spitfire in August 1940. Wolfram became a seaplane pilot but was killed in action in May 1940 whilst dropping mines into Boulogne harbour. Reimar operated as a flight instructor at Köln and his commanding officer, Oskar Dinort, was a keen glider pilot and knew all about the Horten brothers' glider designs and therefore asked Reimar to build one of their Ho IIs for him if he supplied materials, labour and a workplace. Reimar jumped at the chance and as soon as work started other pilots at Köln asked for an example for themselves. This meant that before too long the facility at Köln had enough Horten gliders to enter the flying competition at Wasserkuppe, although they did not perform well due to lack of pilot experience. From 1936 to 1938 Reimar, aided by Walter,

built several II, III and IV gliders, along with the twin-engine all-wing V. Walter's test flight in a captured Spitfire in 1940 convinced him that the only way to build a new fighter superior to the British Spitfire was in the form of an all-wing design. Walter turned down the option of commanding a fighter squadron and instead transferred to Berlin as a technical officer with the Inspection of Fighters Command under the control of Gen. Kurt von Doering. His new job entailed assessing all current and new fighters for the Luftwaffe, as well as knowing about all secret research being carried out, such as the development of the turbojet engine by BMW and Junkers, plus liquid fuel rockets by the likes of Hellmuth Walter, and he was even privy to the new jet-powered fighter being built by Messerschmitt (*See Airframe & Miniature No.1 ©2010*). By 1941 Maj. Oskar Dinort had left

the base at Köln and he was replaced by Maj. Reeps, who had little interest in sailplanes, so Reimar's activities in building gliders was somewhat restricted. Walter came to his rescue and he managed to get Reimar relieved of his flight instructor duties and moved him to a secret Inspection of Fighters special command entitled Sonder-Konnado 3 (the 3 related to Reimar's Ho III design) based at Göttingen. This unit was so secret that its actual purpose was hidden from most, which was just as well, because it was unofficial and totally unauthorised, so Walter was taking a real risk. In August 1941 Walter flew his Bf 108 to Göttingen and collected his brother, then flew to Peenemünde to be present at the first flight of Dr Alexander Lippisch's DFS 194 rocket aircraft; the type would be extensively revised and ordered into production as the Messerschmitt Me 163 (*See Airframe Album No.10 ©2016 ISBN: 978-0-9935345-3-9*). The flight of the DFS 194 had proved to Reimar that Lippisch was much farther advanced then he was with regard to a tailless design capable of exceeding 1,000km/h, and whilst his only concern was now to build such a machine, Walter was thinking more about a new design capable of besting the Allied fighters and bombers. The nature of the rocket motor used by Lippisch in his design was obviously unsuitable for an operational fighter, so both brothers agreed that one of the new turbojet engine designs would be far superior. They also opted for a twin-engine design both to achieve the top speed envisaged and also to give a margin of safety should one engine fail, and Walter was tasked with obtaining the engines, whilst Reimar worked on the new design. A lack of information on the new turbojet designs was initially a problem for Reimar in his design, but Walter obtained an engineering report on the BMW 003 turbojet

The Ho IX V1 outside the garage it was built in prior to movement to the nearby airfield for final assembly; the wing attachment points and the fixed undercarriage are clearly visible

and copied this for his brother, so that he could start working on the new aircraft design. Walter's job meant that he was friends with BMW's director of turbojet research and development, Dr. Hermann Oestrich, and he informed him that the Luftwaffe had ordered the creation of a new all-wing fighter that would use the BMW engines. Oestrich agreed to supply them, but BMW soon stopped all development of the 003 in favour of piston engine production to meet the demands of the Minister of War Production, Albert Speer, so the whole project ground to a halt. BMW did supply two carcases of the 003 engine to the Horten brothers and this allowed Reimar to start work in fitting these within a mock-up of the new type.

Sonder Kommando 3 was terminated by the RLM in March 1943 following the cancellation of their Ho VII project. The situation at this time was such that Nazi Germany was under serous threat, so work continued on the new design, built around the carcasses of the 003s already supplied by BMW. Reimar had decided that he wanted to make two airframes, the Ho IX V1 would be a full-sized unpowered glider, while the V2 would be the first powered prototype. The non-powered version was necessary because Walter had no control and thus access to the wind tunnels used to test new types, as these were controlled by the Civil Air Ministry. Initially Reimar considered fitting a BMW 003 underneath an existing Ho VII airframe, but this was dropped in June 1942 because the type was not strong enough and the underslung nature of the engine would have made it very susceptible to damage due to ingesting stones and dirt during take-off. By early 1943 the Ho IX V1 was nearing completion and work on the V2 continued, when Walter was present at a meeting with Hermann Göring, at which the *Reichsmarschall* decried the mass of twin-engine bombers being produced. He offered 500,000RM to any firm that could submit a fighter-bomber capable of carry 1,000kg of bombs 1,000km at 1,000km/h. After the meeting Walter advised Reimar of

The Horten Ho IX V1 being towed out from the Junkers hangar at Göttingen prior to a test flight. the packed braking parachute can be seen in the bay in the rear of the centre-section

this new requirement and both agreed it was time to submit their proposal for the Ho IX, which they did a few days later by sending it to Göring's chief of staff, Maj. Diesing. The documents were distributed within the RLM, as well as being passed to DFS because Diesing did not believe that Horten could achieve the claimed performance (their designs thus far having reached only 280km/h!) and it took another six months before it was brought before Göring. On the 28th September 1943 Reimar was asked to meet Göring at his Karinhall residence, the

outcome of which was Göring instructing Reimar to build the Ho IX and make it fly. *Generalfeldmarschall* Erhard Milch was also at the meeting and Göring instructed him to issue the 500,000RM, but later when Milch asked Reimar to what firm the payment was to be made, he did not know. He promised details the next day and so the brothers created an incorporated company, Horten Flugzeugbau GmbH, which was awarded the 500,000RM contract to make three prototypes. The initial demands by Göring to have the new type flying in six months was impossible, but Reimar said he would have an unpowered version (the Ho IX VI) ready by the 1st March 1944 and the second powered example by June 1944. The activities of the Horten team were reactivated with the creation of *Luftwaffen-Kommando IX* (*Lw.Kdo.IX*), once again at Göttingen with Hptm. Walter Horten as commander, Oblt. Reimar Horten as his deputy and a workforce that would soon be around 200.

Work on the Ho IX was not without problems though as *Generalfeldmarschall* Milch did not like the design and thought it should not get priority over types such as the Arado Ar 234 (*see Airframe Album No.9 ©2016 ISBN 978-0-9935345-0-8*) and the Dornier Do 335 (*see Airframe & Miniature No.9 ©2016 ISBN: 978-0-9935345-5-3*), so he deliberately side-lined the file and tried to put obstacles in

The Ho IX V1 being towed out of the Junkers hangar at Göttingen on the morning of its maiden flight

its path. Regardless of this and all the other projects the Horten brothers were either designing or actually building, the Ho IX V1 was ready by the 1st March 1944 deadline, although bad weather prevented it flying that day (some sources state it first flew on the 28th February 1944). Other accounts state that the Ho IX V1 undertook a couple of long hops along the airfield at Göttingen, towed by a Heinkel He 46, but it did not have the power to get it fully into the air, so the Hortens requested a Heinkel He 111 tow-plane from the RLM and this was later supplied. The first true flight of the Ho IX V1 was on the 5th March 1944 with Oblt. Heinz Scheidhauer at the controls. After a rather bumpy take-off behind the He 111 he released the tow cable at 3,600m and glided back to Göttingen. His approach meant he had to come over a hangar, so was at quite a steep angle when over the actual runway, this resulted in the aircraft 'floating' and not actually touching down until about halfway along the runway. The braking parachute proved insufficient to slow the aircraft down enough on the snowy ground, so Scheidhauer elected to retract the nose wheel instead of running into a hangar. The Ho IX V1 was later flown by Walter, who felt that the design was not stable enough for a good gun platform and would thus need modification. By March 1944 Walter felt that a small vertical fin and rudder on the back of the Ho IX would cure the oscillation experienced, however his brother would hear none of it; in all likeliness had the war continued, some of the Ho IXs being built by Gotha would have been fitted with a small vertical fin and rudder. Two further tests took place with the Ho IX V1 on the 23rd March 1944, then it moved to Orabuenburg airfield near Berlin with its concrete runways. It was here on the 5th April 1944 that it suffered another accident, this time the nose wheel collapsing after it started to oscillate ('shimmy') during landing. The nose wheel was thereafter modified with torque scissor links and it was test flown again on the 20th April 1944 before being returned to Göttingen. The airframe was fitted out with instrumentation from the *Deutsche Versuchanstalt für Luftfahrt* (DVL) at Berlin-Adlershof for tests relating to stability and control tests. The test report later stated that the type developed a Dutch-roll type lateral/directional oscillation at low speeds.

Supply of the BMW 003 engines was still a problem and Dr. Oestrich suggested that they would be better approaching Dr. Anselm Franz at Junkers, which Walter did and found him very co-operative. The war situation was such though that getting two Jumo 004s to Horten would not be possible until March 1944, however he did supply the carcase of a time-expired 004 engine for them to use. Although the overall size of the 003 and 004 was similar, some modifications were required to the centre section to mount the new engine type and the original air intakes

In this shot taken of the Ho IX V1 in the summer of 1944, here you get to see it from the port rear with the two inboard control surfaces slightly deflected and the braking parachute in situ

The Ho IX V1 in flight for the first time with Heinz Scheidhauer at the controls. Although not clear in this print, it is under tow as the cable can just be seen attached below the nose

The Ho IX V1 after the nose wheel was retracted to stop it hitting a hangar; Reimar Horten looks into the cockpit to assess damage, while Hans Züber (pilot) inflates an airbag to raise the aircraft

The Ho IX V1 with a Horten employee looking into the cockpit to determine damage after the nose wheel deliberately retracted on landing to avoid a collision at Göttingen

situated just below the inboard leading edge of the wing were dispensed with, as it was thought that the slightly curved air intake may have caused disturbance in the air supply. In mid-April 1944 two airworthy Jumo 004B-1 engines were supplied to the Horten brothers and they were dismayed to find the engine had ancillary equipment mounted above the compressor stage, which took it from 60cm (as per the 003) to 80cm diameter and it would therefore simply not now fit between the spar booms. To overcome this the ancillary equipment had to be removed for the engines to be installed, but an easier option was to rotate the engine 90°, so that the ancillary equipment all fitted within the existing airframe. This was approved by Junkers, but for some reason the RLM refused. The only option was therefore to increase the thickness of the wing to accommodate the engine and increase the span from 16m to 21.3m, thus increasing the surface area from 42m2 to 75m2, making the type as large as a conventional bomber and unlikely to achieve the projected top speed. It was far too late to make such modifications to the V2, so instead the outer wings remained unchanged but the centre section wing root would be enlarged by 1m and an additional wing rib would be added to increase the root thickness. The engines were rotated 15° and the annular tank for the starting engine and the oil tank/cooler in front of the engine were all removed (the latter necessitating its relocation). The V2 centre section was stripped and a new larger version (2.4m increased to 3.2m wide and 6.5m increased to 7.47m long) in tubular steel was created. It was claimed this was to accommodate the engines, but the Ho IX V1 actually already had this wider centre section and it was probably initially created to accommodate the proposed cannon armament. These revisions would, it was hoped, reduce the need for the ballast fitted due to the revised CofG with the new engines, but it did not entirely do so and the Ho IX V2 needed 232kg of lead ballast.

A USAAF bombing raid in May 1944 just missed the workshop and so the brothers

The Ho IX V1 was used to test the pressure suit developed by Noble-Dynamit AG and is seen with its very 'Flash Gordon' style helmet on a Horten employee seated in the V1 – this suit was never adopted

decided to move the whole operation to Minden. With no ability to test the revisions made to the V2 it was decided to test some of the features via modified Ho II sailplanes, and test flights with them proved that the changes had little adverse effect on the aerodynamics of the original V2 layout. All

of these factors delayed the first flight of the Ho IX V2 until December 1944, but as it weighed around 7 tons, their existing test pilot, Oblt. Heinz Scheidhauer, was unable to undertake the test because he was only qualified to fly single-engine fighters (regardless of the fact he had flown the twin-engine

The Ho IX V1 in a hangar used by JG400 at Brandis when overrun by the US 9th Armoured Division in 1945 (©US Army)

Ho VII). Although Reimar had wanted to employ Hannan Reitsch to test the Ho IX V2, she was awaiting Dr Lippisch's delta design in Vienna, so they therefore engaged Lt. Erwin Ziller,. He undertook all-wing flight training with the Ho II, IIIb, IIIf and IV sailplanes during May/June 1944, then he undertook powered all-wing flights in the Ho IIId and VII in early December 1944. This was followed at Oranienburg with gliding flights in the Ho IX V1 on the 11th, 16th and 22nd December. The Ho IX V2 had been moved to Oranienburg airfield on the 17th December 1944 and was prepared for its first flight. The actual date on which this took place is in doubt, as fifty years later Reimar thought it was on the 18th December 1944, before he went home for the holidays, however Ziller's flight logs include no flights for that day and only have Ho IX flights listed on the 23rd December? The Rechlin detachment at Oranienburg on that day stated that ground-running of the engines took place on the Ho IX V2, so if this was followed by taxy runs, short hops or even a flight, is unknown but unlikely with Reimar not on site at that time. Ziller actually only undertook jet training on the 29th December 1944, when he flew an Me 262B of the E-Stelle Rechlin from Lärz airfield, followed by solo flights in an Me 262A on the 30th and 31st December, so it seems unlikely the first Ho IX flight was prior to this. Flights of the Ho IX V2 were forbidden by Reimar until he returned after the Christmas break.

Throughout the holiday period the brothers worked on a new all-wing bomber proposal in response to the RLM's Technical Director Col. Siegfried Knemeyer's visit to Göttingen and his test flight in the Ho VII. This new design (Ho XVIII) would have been used for the dropping of an atomic bomb

The Ho IX V1 was never evaluated or ultimately preserved, as seen here in this image of its wreck at Kassel-Rothwesten airfield in 1945

The Ho IX V2 centre-section (2nd version) with empty BMW 003 engines in situ. The original style oval intakes built into the wing leading edge can be clearly seen

The Ho IX V2 centre-section in its third incarnation with empty Jumo 004Bs in place of the original BMW 003s

on the USA and work on the design was top secret, so the Horten brothers were unable to tell the crews waiting for their return at Oranienburg why they suddenly seemed to have lost all interest in testing the Ho IX V2. The Ho IX V2 therefore remained untested at Oranienburg until the 2nd February 1945, when it was at last cleared for flight and Ziller took off to make a 30 minute flight when a speed of 300km/h was achieved with the undercarriage down. The aircraft took to the air again with Ziller at the controls the next day, but it suffered a hard landing due to the premature deployment of the landing parachute; repairs delayed the next flight for two weeks. The third flight with Ziller at the controls was to measure rate of climb and speeds at altitudes up to 4,000m. Just prior to this flight on the 18th February 1945, the V2 had been fitted with FuG 15 radio, but contact with the control tower was not established during the flight. Early in the day the cloud base was at about 500m, but by 2:15pm the cloud covering had decreased enough for Ziller to take off. Climbing at 35°

This starboard side view of the Ho IX V2 being built in a three-car garage. You can clearly see how far above the surface the Jumo 004s now sit

encountered in a dogfight, where its pilot was either dead or unconscious. Why Ziller did not have an oxygen mask on, or had opened the canopy slightly to clear the fumes, will never be known.

In the five-day period after the loss of the V2 all the Horten personnel and equipment left the Oranienburg airfield and returned to Göttingen, as Russian troops were fast approaching. By this stage, both brothers knew that the war was coming to a close, so Reimar was thinking about potential post-war opportunities in Great Britain or the USA, but the loss of the only complete Ho IX meant all that was now in doubt. Neither the RLM nor Göring were concerned about the loss of the V2 though, as flight testing of new designs often resulted in crashes and loss of life, so their interest in the Ho IX remained. The Ho IX V1 was also damaged around this time, when Siegfried Knemeyer crash-landed it, resulting in damage to the undercarriage,

he disappeared into cloud, then came back along a predefined course south of the airfield so that a team from Rechlin could measure the V2's speed and height. Through gaps in the cloud a speed of 795kph was measured but a height of no more than 2,000m was managed. After about 45 minutes the aircraft descended through cloud to the north of the airfield at about 800m and with the starboard engine dead. Ziller attempted to air-start the engine by diving and pulling up a number of times, but this dropped his altitude to 500m. The hydraulic pump that operated the landing gear and flaps was on the engine that had stopped and for some reason Ziller deployed both via the emergency compressed air system well before clearing the railway embankment that ran along the east side of the airfield (the direction he was ultimately going to be approaching from). The increased drag caused the aircraft to drop again and Ziller attempted to gain airspeed by increasing revs on the remaining engine and flying straight and level for a period. This did not work, so he entered a right-hand circling turn with 20° of bank, but as the aircraft entered the second circle the nose dropped and the angle of bank increased still further. On entering the fourth circle the aircraft struck the ground at about a 35° angle some 50m from the railway embankment and both engines and the pilot were thrown clear. Sadly Ziller struck a large tree in the garden of the railway-crossing serviceman's house and was killed instantly. The aircraft did not catch fire as many post-war accounts will state (the remains almost certainly being found post-war by American forces – see elsewhere). Walter believed that fumes from the dead engine had entered the cockpit (there were no bulkheads between the engines and cockpit area in the centre section) and Ziller was unconscious, as he had witnessed the same wide series of circles being done by a Hurricane he had

The outer wing panels of the Ho IX V2 being loaded onto a trailer ready to be taken to Oranienburg for re-assembly

The Ho IX V2 at Oranienburg prior to its first flight, the officer in the foreground is Flight-Ing Franz Binder of Rosarious's Flying Circus, which was also based on the airfield

The assembled Ho IX V2 on the runway at Oranienburg in February 1945, with the engines being run up prior to its first flight

so it was shipped back to Göttingen at the end of March 1945 and then moved by train to Brandis airfield. The Ho VII and Ho IX V1 were both at Brandis by the time the war ended, as they were going to be used in a flight training programme for those pilots that would eventually fly the Ho 229 operationally. In February 1945 the RLM had created Jagdgruppe (JG) 400 to train future pilots of the various new types planned to enter service and such training for the Ho 229 was to be undertaken with the piston-engine Ho VII because the type had similar performance characteristics to the Ho IX. Such a training scheme would have required a lot of Ho VIIs (in production they would have become the Ho 226) and it is thought that Klemm may have relinquished their Ho 229 production contract to build these machines instead. I./JG400 was already involved in training pilots to fly the rocket-powered Messerschmitt Me 163 (*See Airframe Album No.10 ©2016 ISBN: 978-0-9935345-3-9*) but by this stage the Me 163 had proved itself far too dangerous to use operationally, so it was involved in training pilots on such types as the Heinkel He 162 (*See Airframe Album No.13 ©2018 ISBN: 978-0-9957773-4-7*), the Me 263 and the Ho 229. None of these plans came to fruition though as the war ended before the latter two types reached production, even though I./JG54 was planned to be operational with the Ho 229 by August/September 1945.

Planned Production

In June 1944, after the Allied landings in France, the SS started to plan a more central role in Nazi Germany and as a result they looked towards having their own air force, furnished with 'ultimate solution' radical designs. The Ho IX fitted nicely into their plans, so following a meeting with SS representatives on the 15th June 1944, the RLM quickly ordered off the drawing board, ten Ho IXs. To this end thirty SS men from the Oranienburg detachment were made subordinate to Walter Horten and remained with Kommando IX until the end of the war. This initial order for ten aircraft, soon increased to twenty, was placed with Klemm Technik

The centre-section of the Ho IX V3 as found by American troops on the 14th April 1945. Once again it seems to have been being built in a multi-car garage (©USAF)

The Ho IX V3 viewed from the rear at Friedrichroda on capture in April 1945 (©USAF)

at Stuttgert-Böbingen, with an additional twenty aircraft to be made by Gotha Waggon-fabrik. Klemm were already struggling with production of the Me 163, so they sub-contracted the Ho IX order to the large furniture manufacturer May GmbH at Stuttgart-Tamm, who had made Kl 35 wings and other wooden parts. By September though the order with May GmbH was restricted to just making Ho IX wings, all actual production shifting to Gotha. In June 1944 a team of Horten employees led by draughtsman Hans Brüne were sent to Gotha, here they started work in July 1944 on the production version of the Ho IX design, now allocated the next type number in the RLM list ('8.229'). The USAAF Eighth Air Force bombed the Gotha factory on the 20th July 1944 and some 80% was destroyed, so from then on production was dispersed to various sites: Friedrichroda, Goldbach, Wangerenheim, Luisenthal, Wandersleben, Ohrdruf and in a railway depot of Mitropa AG on the Südstrasse in Gotha.

Redesign work on the Ho IX to create the new production '8.229' required the removal of the original spring-loaded ejection seat, as it offered little acceleration, so an alternative type was sought from Dornier (as used in their Do 335). The Watanzug flying suit designed by Dräger was also ground-tested in

Found along with the Ho IX V3 at Friedrichroda was the partially complete Ho IX V4 (©USAF)

Lt Erwin Ziller, the pilot of the Ho IX V2, who was sadly killed during a test flight on the 18th February 1945

the Ho IX V1, but it was found to be too late to redesign the Ho IX cockpit and so it was rejected for the production version. The Ho IX V3 (often listed as the 8.229 V3) was subject to a complete redesign of the Jumo 004B engine installation complete with standard circular tanks for the oil and starter motor fuel, thus shifting the entire installation slightly forward. The relocated engines projected above the upper surface of the wing, but this did allow a revision to the original 13% thickness at the junction with the outer wing panels. To cool the Jumo 004 it had its own built-in bleed air nozzles, but the steel plates aft of the exhausts were also cooled via a gap between them and the actual ply

skin, fed with air taken from the underside of each wing. The nose wheel was revised using a 1015 x 380mm wheel with double brakes and ex-Bf 109 740mm x 210mm main wheels (with the oleo legs inclined inwards to ensure the tyre was vertical). The larger nose wheel increased the angle with the ground, thus making take-off possible with little or no rotation. The controls were also simplified, with single-stage brake rudder and elevons that had the inner sections doubling as landing flaps. Even with all these changes, the type still needed 300kg of ballast to allow the rearmost permissible CofG. As all these changes still would not make the 8.229 ready for series production it was decided to build the first three prototypes to the same standard

as the 8.229 V3 and the V3, V4 and V5 were therefore entitled *Göttinger Ausführungen* (Göttinger versions'). The V6 to V15 would be to production standards and a preliminary description of the V6 was prepared in mid-November 1944.

The V4 and V5 airframes were to have served as prototypes for the proposed two-seat nightfighter version envisaged for production as the Ho 229B-1 and this type would have used the new FuG 244 Bremen airborne interception radar (Horten prepared the design in February 1945). The V6 was to have been the second single-seat A-series airframe and would have had a pressurised cockpit, FuG 16ZY radio (later replaced by the newer FuG 15) and FuG 25a (IFF) and FuG 125

This is a rear view of the partially complete Ho IX V4 found at Friedrichroda – note that a shadow of the windscreen surround on the back wall may make some think this was one of the two-seat prototypes!

The Ho IX V3 being unloaded at Freeman Field in August 1945 (©H. Furst via Internet)

interest that Gen McDonald, the Director of US Strategic Air Force Intelligence, recommended it be moved to Mersburg some 20km west of Leipzig, where a US Air Technical Intelligence collection point was situated. The Americans also learned of the location of two drums of drawings hidden by Horten at Friedrichroda and these were subsequently retrieved along with another Ho IX that was in a barn at Rodach near Coburg. This latter aircraft's location was discovered during interrogation of the Horten brothers by the RAE in the UK and it was almost certainly the remains of the V2. This was later loaned by Gen. McDonald to Capt. Eric Brown and shipped to the UK in August 1945 in the hold of a captured Arado Ar 232. Although initially intended to be restored to flight, this never happened and it was eventually sent to the USA in the mid-1945 or 1946 although its ultimate fate is unknown. American reports also state that another flying wing was found in a shed at Friedrichroda, where about 1/2km away there had been a remote Gotha assembly facility in a railway tunnel, and this aircraft was apparently removed by the Americans although what it actually was and what happened to it is unknown. The V3 and V4 were moved to a US Air Technical Intelligence packing and crating centre code-named 'Gunfire' in a village called Wolfgang (now part of Hanau) near Frankfurt. At the end of May 1945 the unit was instructed to

(homing device), along with either four MK 108 or two MK 103 cannon. Work was quite advanced on the V6 when Friedrichsroda was captured by US forces, but it was subsequently scrapped because the V3 was earmarked for evaluation and the Allies apparently had little interest in all-wing designs for military purposes by mid-1945. The V7 was to have been a two-seat trainer version, but it was never completed and the V8 was to have been the third pre-production A-series airframe with all operational equipment installed, but it is unlikely work was ever started on it. A bomber version of the Ho 229 was to have had a pylon under each wing allowing it to carry two 500kg SD bombs on ETC 501 *Wikingerschiff* racks, while the reconnaissance version would have had two Rb 20/30, Rb 50/30 or Rb 75/30 cameras installed in place of the cannon in the port wing, thus leaving just two MK 108s with 90rpg in the starboard wing. It is likely that the latter design would have also needed to carry a 300lt drop tank under each wing, but the changing situation with the war by 1945 was such that many potential modifications were envisaged for future aircraft designs, many of which were never recorded, so there may have been various other layouts envisaged for the Ho 229.

Survivor

Col. George Patton's Third Army, VII Corps found three (some sources state four) Horten flying wing centre sections in the Gotha dispersal factory at Friedrichroda, known as Ortlepp Model Fabrik, on the 14th April 1945. One of these was the Ho IX V3 and it was eventually crated and shipped to the USA as part of 'Operation Seahorse'. The wings were found in a different location some 120km from Friedrichroda by the US Air Dis-

armament Division, Ninth Air Force Service Command (this was most likely the Robert Hartwig Co. at Sonneberg) and shipped separately from the centre section. Found along with the V3 was the partially built V4 and the centre section framework of the V6 (many list this as the V5, but period images

The Ho IX V3 centre-section photographed at Freeman Field not long after its arrival in August 1945 (©USAF)

show it to be a single-seater and the V5 was to have been a two-seater, like the V4). The V6 subsequently disappeared from all records and it is thought it was scrapped. The Ho IX V1 had been captured at Leipzig-Brandis airfield on the 6th May 1945 by the US 9th Armoured Division and although damaged it was considered of sufficient technical

ship the flying wings to American, but it was decided to leave the incomplete V4 behind and it was probably subsequently scrapped there. Interest in the Horten brothers and their flying wings suddenly waned in late June 1945 and they were considered of little interest to military intelligence. The Ho IX V1 and V3 were at this stage being prepared for

A port side view of the Ho IX V3 centre-section at Freeman Field in August 1945, this photograph is the one that started my whole fascination with Luftwaffe projects, when I saw it in a book I was given when at Primary School – I wish I could find a large format, good quality version to frame and hang up in the office! (©USAF)

shipment to the USA, but this was stopped and the V1 was abandoned and later burned at Kassel-Rothwestern airfield. The V3 had been moved down the autobahn to Kassel on the 20-22 June 1944, probably to join the V1 for its intended shipment to the USA, and on the 26th June 1945 it was moved by train to Cherbourg, where it was loaded on the Liberty Ship SS Richard J. Gatling and sailed to the USA on the 12th July 1945. The centre section and one incomplete (starboard) wing eventually arrived by train at Freeman Field, Indiana in early August 1945. Once in the USA it was allocated Foreign Evaluation (FE) number 490 (changed in early 1946 to T2-490) and it was displayed, along with the incomplete wing, to the press and general public within the hangars at Freeman Field in

November 1945. By January 1946 the return of the aircraft to flight was considered too costly as it would require a major re-design, so it was rejected. By 16th May 1946 it was listed as being just in storage at Freeman Field and although some sources state it eventually ended up at Wright-Patterson Air Base in Dayton, Ohio, that is unlikely as the assessment of 15,000 man hours to make it airworthy was probably made by Air Force officials from Wright-Patterson detached to Freeman Field, so that explains the confusion. By August 1946 the V3 was being renovated for display purposes, both wings were by this stage present and both were covered with low-grade plywood of reduced thickness and then the whole thing was painted with spurious camouflage and markings (including

huge swastikas above the tail region). With the closure of Freeman Field in the summer of 1946 the V3 was moved to No.803 Special Depot at Park Ridge, Illinois (it is here that photographs exist showing the airframe assembled with its wing). Here it was stored with around eighty WWII aircraft in the former Douglas Aircraft Co. facility at Orchard airfield (now O'Hare International Airport) and was earmarked for use in the proposed Air Force Technical Museum. In September 1947 all these airframes were transferred to the National Air Museum, which was part of the Smithsonian Institute established in 1946 (later to become the National Air and Space Museum in 1966). With the Douglas Aircraft Co. facility at Park Ridge re-activated for C-119 assembly due to the Korean War,

This photograph proves that the Ho IX V3 was assembled with its wings whilst in storage facility in the Douglas factory in Chicago (©R. Kik Jr via Internet)

The Ho IX V3 centre-section being moved by road from Silver Hill to the Mary Baker Engen Restoration Center of NASM's Steven F. Udvar-Hazy Center at Dulles airport in 2012 (©NASM)

all of the aircraft stored there were nearly scrapped, but thanks to the work of the the National Air Museum's curator (Paul E. Garber), most of the aircraft (sadly not all) were saved with some being moved to a wooded area near Silver Hill, Maryland in 1952. Most of the larger aircraft (including the V3) were unable to be placed in the limited hangar space, so they remained outside in the elements for more than a decade.

The V3 remained in storage for the next sixty years until it was transferred from Building 22 at the Paul E. Garber storage facility, Silver Hill to the Mary Baker Engen Restoration Center in late 2012. Here it was assessed and remedial conservation action was undertaken to arrest areas of corrosion on metal and distortion and delamination of the wooden components. After this was completed the unrestored aircraft, with the wings unattached and on a separate trolley, was moved into the Boeing Aviation Hangar at the Steven F. Udvar-Hazy Center at Dulles airport, where it can be seen today. Although the type has been scheduled for restoration on many occasions, the airframe will remain untouched for at least the next decade while NASM completely renovates and upgrades its downtown museum facility in Washington D.C.

Specifications – Go 229 V3	
Span:	16.8m
Length:	7.465m
Height:	2.9m (others state 2.81m)
Weight:	Take-off 7,515kg
Engines:	Two Junkers Jumo 004B-2 axial compressor turbojets offering 890kg thrust

Performance (calculated)

Max. Speed: 840km/h

Note that there are many other performance figures quoted in various published sources for the Go 229, however all of these are projected (calculated) as no such data was ever established with the type because only the V2 ever flew.

Armament:	None fitted
Radio:	None fitted

Note: We have refrained from making conversions from Metric to Imperial as far as dimensions go, as these would always be approximations at best and as the type was built to the Metric standard, we have included just those dimensions in the above specifications

The Ho IX V3 centre-section, with its wings on a stand alongside, on display in the Boeing Hangar of the Steven F. Udvar-Hazy Center at Dulles airport (©Scott Willey)

Section 1

Technical Description

What follows is an extensive selection of images and diagrams that will help you understand the physical nature of the Ho IX/Ho 229.

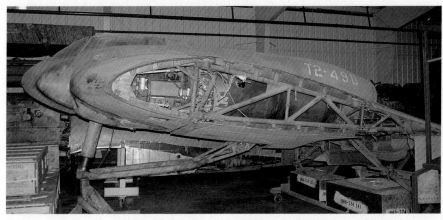

Ho 229 port side over at Silver Hill (Scott Willey)

Please note that the Ho 229 never entered series production, nor was it built in sufficient numbers for pre-production machines to undertake service trials. As a result there were never any flight or spare parts manuals produced for the type, so we are unable to offer the usual black & white artwork from such official publications in this section. The only such artwork can be found in post-war British and American evaluation reports of the Horten designs, and these often combined original (and redrawn) Horten diagrams with newly drawn illustrations made after evaluation of the captured Ho IX V2 (components) and V3 (airframe).

A front view of the V3 with its wings alongside in the Boeing Hall of the Steven F. Udvar-Hazy Center (©Scott Willey)

Another view of the V3 centre section at the Steven F. Udvar-Hazy Center (©Scott Willey)

An overall shot of the V3, with wings alongside and He 219 fuselage and wings (now re-assembled) behind (©Scott Willey)

1.1 Cockpit Interior

This photograph is often quoted as having been taken of the V3's cockpit interior at Freeman Field in mid-1945, however the jack just visible in the top right hand corner and the lack of the leading edge fairing on the starboard side means this was taken not long after its capture in April 1945 at Gotha's Ortlepp Model Fabrik facility *(©US Army)*

1. Turn and bank indicator
2. Repeater compass
3. Vertical speed indicator
4. ASI
5. Altimeter (missing)
6. AFN2 direction finder indicator
7. Undercarriage position indicator
8. Ignition breakers, port/ starboard engines
9. Flap position indicator (top to bottom: landing, take-off, up)
10. Emergency circuit breaker
11. Hydraulic pressure gauge (missing)
12. Oil pressure gauges
13. Exhaust temperature gauges
14. RPM indicators
15. Oxygen pressure gauge
16. Oxygen indicator
17. Ambient temperature gauge
18. Fuel gauges
19. Low fuel warning indicators
20. Canopy emergency jettison handle (port one is missing)
21. Throttle
22. Canopy rail
23. Canopy fixing stub
24. Ejection seat lever
25. Rudder pedals (with toe brakes)
26. Control column height adjustment lever
27. Control column (top section missing)
28. Air brake release lever

A period image of the interior of the cockpit in the Ho IX V1, viewed from the port, rear

This is how the V3's interior looks today, as seen here during assessment and remedial conservation work at the Mary Baker Engen Restoration Center (©NASM)

A close-up of the upper and starboard corners of the main instrument panel in the V3, with pretty much all the flight instruments removed from the centre of the panel (©Scott Willey)

This is the port side of the main instrument panel, plus you can just see the throttle controls on the left – the exposed spring is a buffer for the canopy

(©Scott Willey)

This shows the lower front area of the starboard sidewall in the V3, the handle at the back/middle is linked to the seat ejection system *(©Scott Willey)*

This is an overall view of the starboard sidewall in the V3 *(©Scott Willey)*

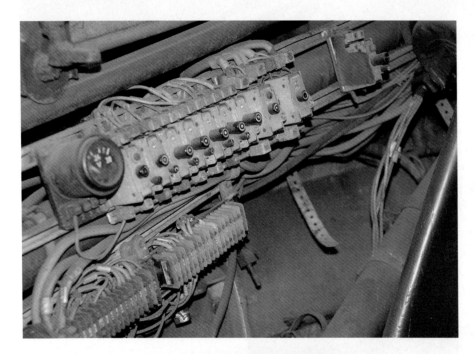

A close look at the starboard sidewall in the V3 highlights the electrical distribution (fuse) panel in this area, with the voltmeter on the far left

(©Scott Willey)

The rearmost corner of the starboard sidewall, the cylindrical item may be a transformer *(©Scott Willey)*

The port side of the V3's interior, the control column in the foreground has always been without the top – see the 1945 image elsewhere *(©Scott Willey)*

Looking aft on the port side you can see the fuel pressure gauge and two fuel tank (electrical) switches. You can also see the roller and runner at the top for the sliding canopy *(©Scott Willey)*

This is the upper portion of the seat in the V3, it's not a true ejection seat, more of an 'assisted' unit using a charge to accelerate it rather than rockets *(©Scott Willey)*

Moving down towards the front of the seat you can see the foot rests plus how the top of the nose oleo leg is right underneath – the area would have been open(!), so the pilot could see down through when the undercarriage was lowered *(©Scott Willey)*

1.2 Canopy

Heinz Scheidhauer entering the cockpit of the Ho IX V1

An overall view of the nose area of the Ho IX V1, showing the smooth lines of the canopy as well as details such as the pitot under the port and venturi under the starboard wing leading edges

An overall view from the front of the windscreen and sliding canopy of the V3 during conservation work in 2012-2019 (©NASM)

This is the sliding canopy section of the V3 removed during conservation work, you can clearly see the wooden rear decking area and side frames, only the frame around the Perspex is metal (©Scott Willey)

In this higher view of the V3's canopy you can see the elongated area behind the glazed sliding portion. The oblong hole in the port side seems to be original, as it can be seen in images of the centre section at Freeman Field in 1945, so it was most likely intended to have a hinged clear panel added to it to allow ventilation of the cockpit interior; see the image later of the pressure suit tests, as that shows the hinged panel in the V1's canopy (©NASM)

Back in the days when the V3 was still at Silver Hill, here with the main canopy slid back you can see the roller at its front edge that goes along the tube in the top of each sidewall (©Scott Willey)

These two period views show a Horten employee wearing the pressure suit developed by Noble-Dynamit AG – this was only tested here in the Ho IX V1, as it was never adopted for operational use

2.1 Centre-section

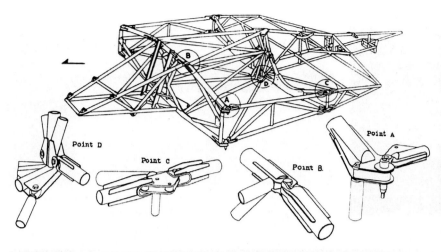

This period diagram can be found in Allied post-war evaluation documents, so is most likely ex-Horten or redrawn from the same, and it shows the tubular construction of the centre-section

The V3 centre section undergoing conservation work, and with the all the metal elements off you can see the structure around the engines and cockpit *(©Scott Willey)*

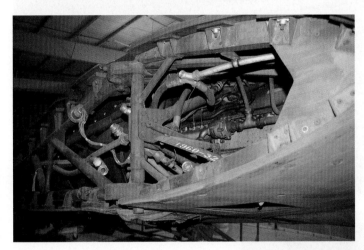

This is the leading edge region of the starboard wing root, note the metal fixings but wooden nose ribs and the forward spar pick-ups in the tubular structure *(©Scott Willey)*

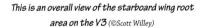

This is an overall view of the starboard wing root area on the V3 *(©Scott Willey)*

This is the rear wing spar pick-up on the starboard side of the V3 *(©Scott Willey)*

This is a closer view, from the rear, of the front spar pick-up on the starboard wing of the V3 *(©Scott Willey)*

The rearmost area of the wing root on the V3, with the trailing edge supported via solid tapered blocks of wood to which the outer skin is nailed and glued (©Scott Willey)

A slightly elevated view of the rear spar pick-up on the starboard side in which you can also see the plywood skins, which are original on the centre section and clearly show the delamination and rot that has occurred after 60+ years of storage (©Scott Willey)

Here you have an overall view of the wing root on the port side of the V3 (©Scott Willey)

Here is a close-up of the front region of the port wing root on the V3 (©Scott Willey)

A closer look at the forward region on the port wing root of the V3 shows the various engine related pipework and electrical connections in that area (©Scott Willey)

Here you can see the mid and rear section of the port wing root on the V3, this area really only contains the rear spar pick-ups (©Scott Willey)

Moving forward, this is the nose section of the V3, which was all laminated and shaped plywood, made in two halves *(©Scott Willey)*

Moving back to the starboard side, now viewed underneath though, you can see the various panels that go around the wing leading edge to create the engine intakes in metal (rust being very evident on these) and the laminated plywood that is used to form the leading edge profile *(©Scott Willey)*

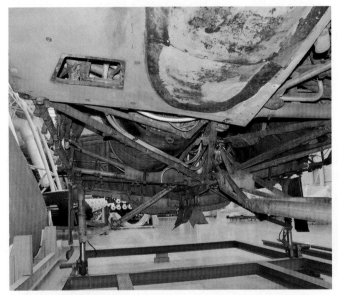

If you turn around from the previous location this is the area under the starboard side looking aft with the lower (plywood) panels all removed exposing the engine and undercarriage with all the associated pipework etc. *(©Scott Willey)*

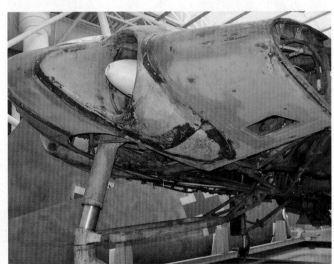

This view under the front of the port side again shows the (rusty) metal cowls around the engine intakes, the (plywood) leading edge profile and the structure exposed underneath where the (plywood) access panels have been removed *(©Scott Willey)*

Here is a view looking back underneath the port side of the V3, which is pretty much a mirror image of the starboard *(©Scott Willey)*

This is a view of the underside from the back on the port side of the V3, with the nose leg and struts visible in the distance and the retraction arms for the main wheels in the foreground *(©Scott Willey)*

A difficult area to reach and photograph, this is the area directly behind the cockpit with the cover removed and viewed from the rear (©Scott Willey)

Moving the camera out a bit from the previous shot, here you can see the area in relation to the engines on either side and the rear decking in the middle (©Scott Willey)

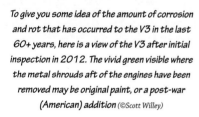

To give you some idea of the amount of corrosion and rot that has occurred to the V3 in the last 60+ years, here is a view of the V3 after initial inspection in 2012. The vivid green visible where the metal shrouds aft of the engines have been removed may be original paint, or a post-war (American) addition (©Scott Willey)

The huge swastikas on either side of the upper surface of the tail are not original, they, like all the overall colours and markings, were added at Freeman Field in 1946 when the airframe was refurbished for display purposes (©Scott Willey)

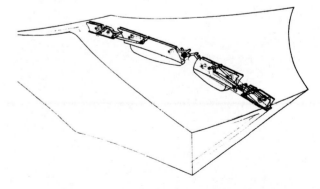

The Ho IX/Ho 229 would have had a series of dive brakes fitted aft of the wheel wells in the centre section underside, this period diagram shows such an installation although it is impossible to know if this relates to the V1 or V2, or both?

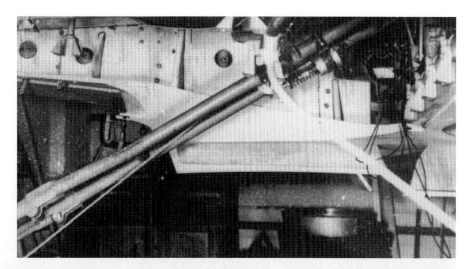

This is the only known period image that shows
the dive brakes under the Ho IX V2

This is a view of the dive brakes under the V3, viewed from the rear
on the starboard side (©Scott Willey)

This is a view of the V3's dive brakes from further aft on the
starboard side (©Scott Willey)

One of the ventral access panels, which
is wooden and does not look too bad
from a distance (©Scott Willey)

Up close you can see the damage caused by water, which has seeped into the
airframe during the last 60+ years (some of which was in outside storage) and
has then set about delaminating the wood, blistering both paint and glue and
corroding any metal fittings (©Scott Willey)

The amount of work required to stabilise and repair such water damage
in wood is such that it is just not viable, so we suspect items like this
would be only used as patterns to make new ones should the V3 ever
go into full restoration (©Scott Willey)

2.2 Engines

The production Ho 229 as well as all prototypes would have been powered by the Junkers Jumo 004, as seen here with one being examined at the Aircraft Engine Research Laboratory, NACA in 1946 – this is probably from an Me 262 going by the front fairing (©NACA)

This period image shows the V2 fitted with the early five-stage compressor stage BMW 003 engines. These were not adopted and as you can see, they initially had the exhausts slightly splayed outwards from one another

This shows a mock-up of the oval intake below the leading edge of the wings in the V2, which once the 004 was adopted was dropped from the design

Although not the best quality, this image shows the oval intakes under the wing leading edge in the V2 when fitted with BMW 003 engines

To install the bigger Jumo 004 engine the intakes were enlarged and became round within the leading edge, as seen here in this initial modification – note that the engine inside lacks the starter unit and as you can see straight through it in the middle, it is a hollow carcase

This photograph taken by US forces at Friedrichroda in 1945 clearly shows the installation of both Jumo 004 engines in the V6 (©USAF)

This is another period image taken by US troops at Friedrichroda in April 1945, this time showing the port engine complete with starter unit in the middle and metal shrouds around the intake (©USAF)

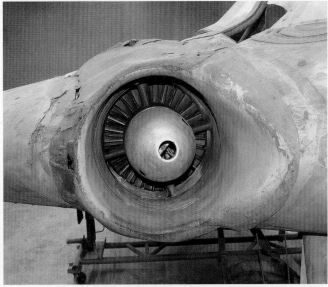

Here is the same area some 60 years later, whilst in store at Silver Hill (©Scott Willey)

During remedial conservation work in 2012 the port intake cover was removed, allowing you to see that the engines were visible from the cockpit, with no bulkheads or firewalls (©Scott Willey)

A look into the port engine whilst undergoing conservation allows you to see the area exposed when the starter motor and its associated cover are removed (©Scott Willey)

When the V3 was captured in April 1945 the port engine lacked the outer fairing, as seen in this period image (©USAF)

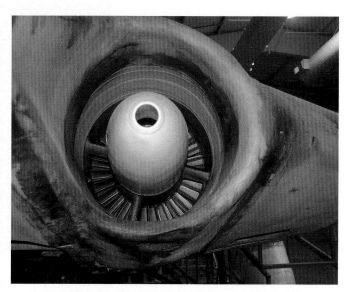

The missing port engine intake fairing was either attached or created prior to its being shipped to the USA and thus was present when it was stored at Silver Hill, as seen here (©Scott Willey)

Once again during conservation work in 2012-2019 the fairing and starter motor was also removed from the port side (©Scott Willey)

Here is an overall view from the front of both engine intakes on the V3 whilst at Silver Hill (©Scott Willey)

During conservation work all the metal and wooden access panels were removed from the V3, here you can see the metal intake cover from the port engine (©Scott Willey)

The starboard intake is in even worse condition, as its upper surfaces are severely corroded (©Scott Willey)

You can see the engine through the wing root, as seen here with the front area on the port side (©Scott Willey)

This close-up of the port engine intake cover gives you some idea of the level of corrosion that has occurred over the years (©Scott Willey)

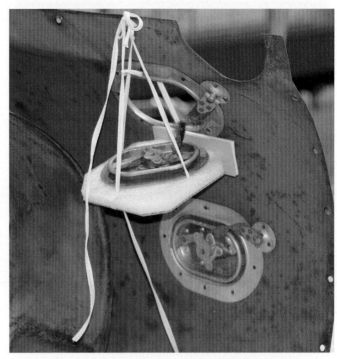

Here you can see the oval access panels in the engine intake cover (port side shown), which are in better shape because they are aluminium, not mild steel like the panel itself (©Scott Willey)

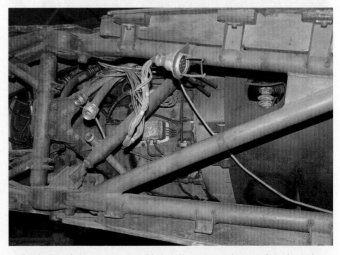

The cluster of connectors you could see in the previous shot are shown here, they mainly consist of hydraulic/pneumatic pipes and a series of electrical wires via a single connector – the mid section of the engine can be seen further back inside

(©Scott Willey)

The mid and rear section of the wing root allow you to see the 'hot' areas of the engines, all of which are covered by metal (curved) shrouds that were painted with a special paint to indicate if they got too hot *(©Scott Willey)*

The rearmost section of the wing root allows little of the engine to be seen, as just the exhaust region is visible on the left with the associated engine fairing visible above *(©Scott Willey)*

On the underside, with the access panels off, this is the front region of the starboard engine *(©Scott Willey)*

While this is the rear section of the engine visible on the starboard underside with the access panels removed *(©Scott Willey)*

An overall view of the exhausts of both engines on the V3 *(©Scott Willey)*

The areas of the upper surface directly behind the exhausts were covered with metal, which drew cold air from the underside of the centre section and vented it through the slots you can see just aft of the swastika *(©Scott Willey)*

Here is a close look into the exhaust of the port Jumo 003 *(©Scott Willey)*

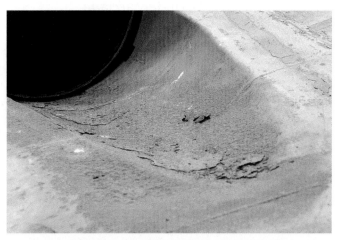

Again, the metal of the shrouds aft of the engines have all suffered from a lot of corrosion, due entirely to their concave shape, which would hold water, not disperse it *(©Scott Willey)*

The upper cowls over each engine can be seen here removed from the airframe during conservation work. They are also steel, but faired a little better than the exhaust panels because they were painted and their curved nature would make water run off

(©Scott Willey)

With the cowls off the engines on the V3 you can see the location of the gearbox (1) and heat sensor (2) shown in detail in the two images below *(©Scott Willey)*

1
2

This is the gearbox situated on the port side of the Jumo engine just before the final exhaust stage *(©Scott Willey)*

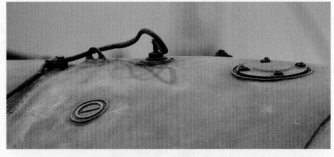

This is the heat sensor's cable and connection into the rearmost section of the Jumo 004, slightly offset to starboard *(©Scott Willey)*

3.1 Nose Undercarriage

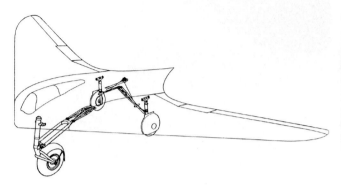

This period diagram used in Allied post-war examination reports shows the overall undercarriage system of the V3 and thus applicable to all single-seat production variants

This is an overall view of the nose leg and wheel fitted to the Ho IX V1 – you can also see the venturi under the starboard and pitot under the port wing leading edges

The nose wheel of the Ho IX V2 came from a wrecked He 177 with the retraction arms etc. new additions

This diagram from the He 177 manual shows in detail the tailwheel unit used by the type and adopted for the Ho IX V2

Extended	Retracted
1. Latch lever	4. Cylinder
4. Retraction jack	5. Tailwheel retraction
8. Lock hook	segment
9. Lock cylinder	6. Tailwheel door
	7. Lock roller
	8. Lock hook
	9. Lock cylinder

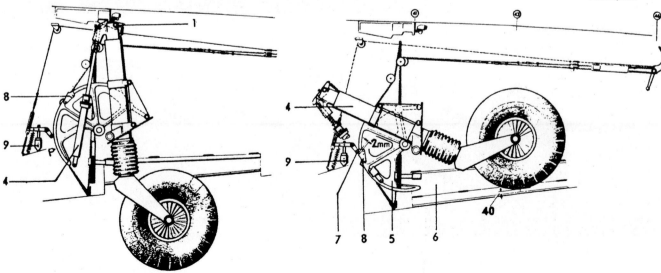

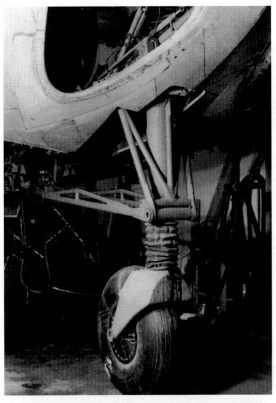

This is the V2's nose leg in the fully retracted position, again without the door installed

This view shows the nose leg of the V2 in the fully extended position but with the door not fitted

The nose leg on the V3 when found in 1945 was completely different from that of the V2, with both an enlarged wheel hub/tyre and revisions to the associated yoke as seen in this period image (©USAF)

This is the nose oleo on the V3 viewed from the port side (©Scott Willey)

This is the V3's nose leg oleo without the wheel, viewed from the starboard side, as seen today on display with NASM (©Scott Willey)

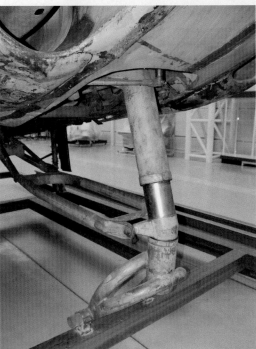

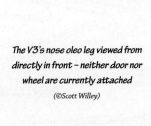

The V3's nose oleo leg viewed from directly in front – neither door nor wheel are currently attached (©Scott Willey)

This is the upper mounting point of the nose oleo leg on the V3 *(©Scott Willey)*

This is an overall view, from the port side, of the V3's nose oleo leg and its associated retraction linkage *(©Scott Willey)*

This is a more detailed view of the aft region of the V3's nose oleo legs retraction arm *(©Scott Willey)*

This shows the rearmost section of the nose oleo retraction linkage, with the hydraulic ram that actuates it just visible *(©Scott Willey)*

With the lower cowls off you can more clearly see the hydraulic ram at the rear of the retraction arm, plus how it mounts onto the centre section framework *(©Scott Willey)*

3.2 Main Undercarriage

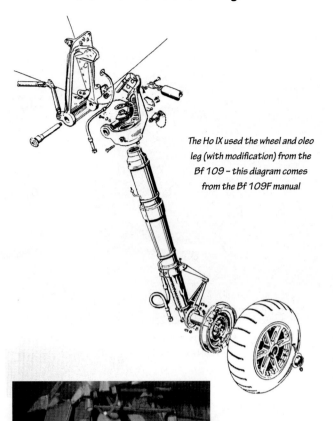

The Ho IX used the wheel and oleo leg (with modification) from the Bf 109 – this diagram comes from the Bf 109F manual

Here you can see the Bf 109 leg installed in an Ho IX, this is either the V1 or V2, as the leg's upper casting was revised on the V3

This is the starboard main oleo of the V3, you can see how it differs from the leg seen in the previous image, the casting at the top now having lugs both fore and aft, whilst the original Bf 109 leg only has a lug at the rear. Note also how the locking yoke at the end of the retraction arms is pulled inboard by a wire, not hydraulics

The starboard main leg of the V3 when captured in April 1945, both main and secondary doors can be seen in place, plus you can also see the access panel in the middle of the secondary door and the up-lock switch on the retraction arm to the right

An overall shot of the starboard main oleo leg on the V3 with NASM, the wheel is no longer fitted and the door is yet to be installed, so the hydraulic line for the brakes can be seen hanging down inboard of the axle

(©Scott Willey)

This is the main door of the port leg on the V3 whilst it was in storage at Silver Hill – the front of the aircraft is to the left (©Scott Willey)

This is a view of the inside of the port undercarriage door, which allows you to see the tubular internal structure and the linkage to the oleo leg itself

(©Scott Willey)

In this view of the starboard leg and door from the rear you can see the linkage arm between the retraction arm and the oleo and how that is then linked to the door *(©Scott Willey)*

This view, again of the port undercarriage, allows you to see the retraction linkage *(©Scott Willey)*

This is the upper area of the starboard wheel well, with the leg and door to the left and the retraction arm to the left – the airframe has none of the lower panels fitted, so you can see the engine etc. up inside *(©Scott Willey)*

Looking inboard in the starboard wheel well, you can see the retraction linkage, how it mounts to the centre section framework and the inner undercarriage doors *(©Scott Willey)*

A close-up of the inner undercarriage doors, which again have tubular interior structure (with holes to reduce weight) and how they mount to the centre section framework. There is no retraction jack, so we suspect that they were linked to the retraction arm, which thus pulled them shut as the linkage arm folded up *(©Scott Willey)*

The wooden structure of the wings means that there is little inside the top of the wheel wells, as seen here in the port bay of the V3, looking aft *(©Scott Willey)*

4.0 Wings

This period photograph shows the wings of the Ho IX V1 during final assembly, with just the outer skins to be attached

The wings of the Ho IX V1 after completion – the fuel cells are visible through the root

A port side view of the inboard spar held by Horten workshop manager Herr Seeboda

A detailed close-up of the spar pick-up points – the black substance is glue

This is an overall view of the top of the Ho IX V2's port wing during construction, showing all the various ribs etc.

Here the leading edge veneer of the V2's port wing is tacked onto the nose ribs

This cross-section diagram of the wing shows the auxiliary fuel tank in the leading edge, the main tank in the rear and the tubes in the centre that contained the control rods etc.

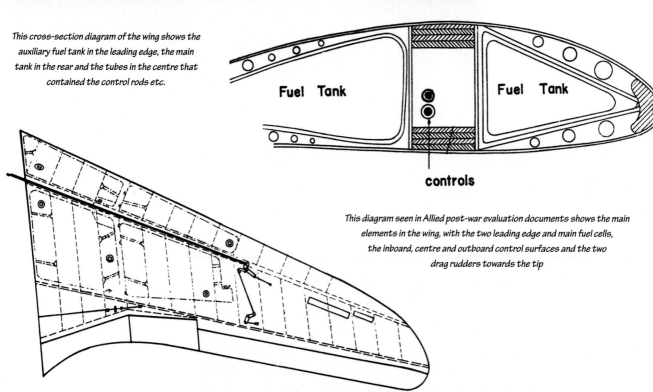

Fuel Tank   Fuel Tank

controls

This diagram seen in Allied post-war evaluation documents shows the main elements in the wing, with the two leading edge and main fuel cells, the inboard, centre and outboard control surfaces and the two drag rudders towards the tip

A period image showing the starboard wing tip with the control surfaces not installed

A view of the wings, on their trolley, whilst the airframe underwent some remedial conservation work – the paint scheme and marking were applied in 1946 at Freeman Field (©Scott Willey)

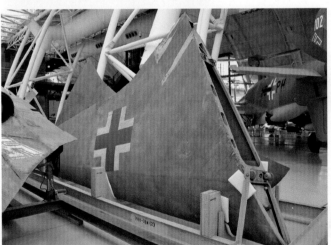

Another view of the wings in their cradle as now displayed by NASM, you can see the spar pick-ups on the end of the nearer port wing, along with the damage to the trailing and leading edges (©Scott Willey)

Damage to the skins on the wing are evident in this shot, the outer plywood on the wings is a post-war addition though, when the wings were refurbished along with the centre section for display at Freeman Field in 1946 (©Scott Willey)

Stacking wings vertical saves space, but if water gets inside this is the result, it pools in the leading edge and eventually rots its way through (©Scott Willey)

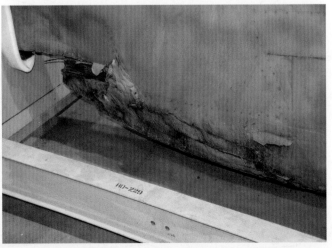

At some stage in the past 60 years the leading edge of the tip of the port wing sustained some severe crush damage, so this region will have to be remanufactured should the type ever be fully restored (©Scott Willey)

This view of the port wing on the stand in the Boeing Hall at NASM clearly shows four of the five mounting points for the elevon (©Scott Willey)

Here is a close-up of one of the five pivot/mounting points for the elevon (©Scott Willey)

Here you can see the outboard last three pivot/mounting points for the elevon on the port wing of the V3 (©Scott Willey)

The outboard control surface doubled as aileron and elevators, hence it being termed as an 'elevon' – note the five cut-outs for the pivot/ mounting points

This diagram shows the inner, mid and outboard control surfaces on the Ho 229's wing, plus the drag rudders towards the tips

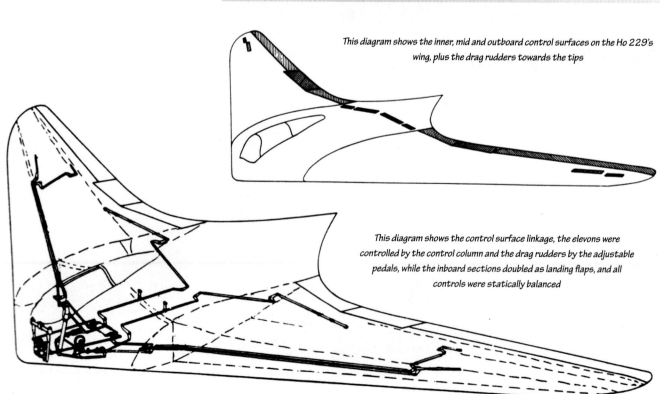

This diagram shows the control surface linkage, the elevons were controlled by the control column and the drag rudders by the adjustable pedals, while the inboard sections doubled as landing flaps, and all controls were statically balanced

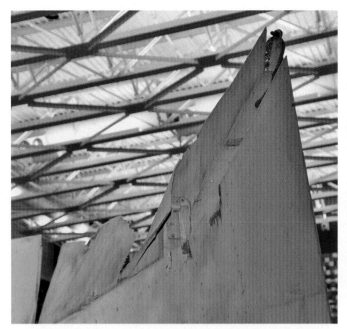

This is the inboard region of the port wing of the V3, with the control surfaces removed you can see the overlapping of the upper skin and the tunnel it creates, plus the very basic mounting points for each control surface *(©Scott Willey)*

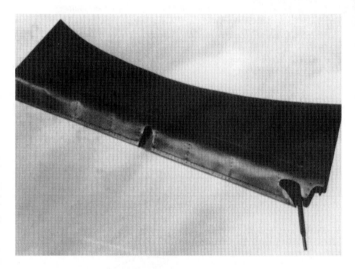

This is the port inner control surface control linkage shaft

This is the port inner control surface, which was used with the middle control surface as landing flaps

This is the second control surface of the centre section (middle flap) with blunt Frise nose and trimming tab

This is the control linkage of the second control surface

The Ho IX/Ho 229 was fitted with two drag rudders above the wing towards each tip – they are seen here in the fully extended position above the port wing

Here are the drag rudders above the port wing, with the inboard one extended slightly

Here is a view of the drag rudder fully deployed above a completed and painted Ho IX wing

One of the auxiliary fuel tanks that fitted into the leading edge of the wing, as used by the Ho IX V2 and V3

This diagram shows the fuel delivery system of the Ho IX V2 and V3

1. Main (discharge) tanks
2, 3 & 4. Auxiliary tanks
5. Electric outboard connection
6. Fuel control panel
7. Pump
8. Back pressure valve
9. Fuel filler point
10. Engines

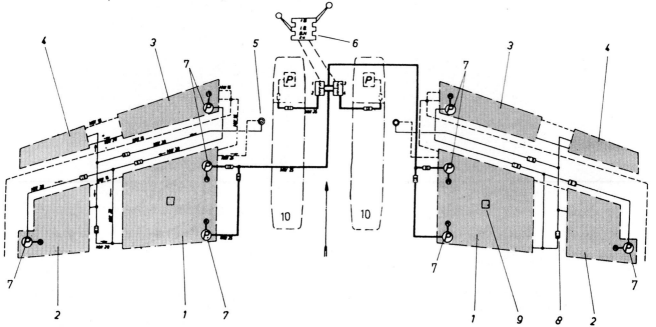

5.1 Armament

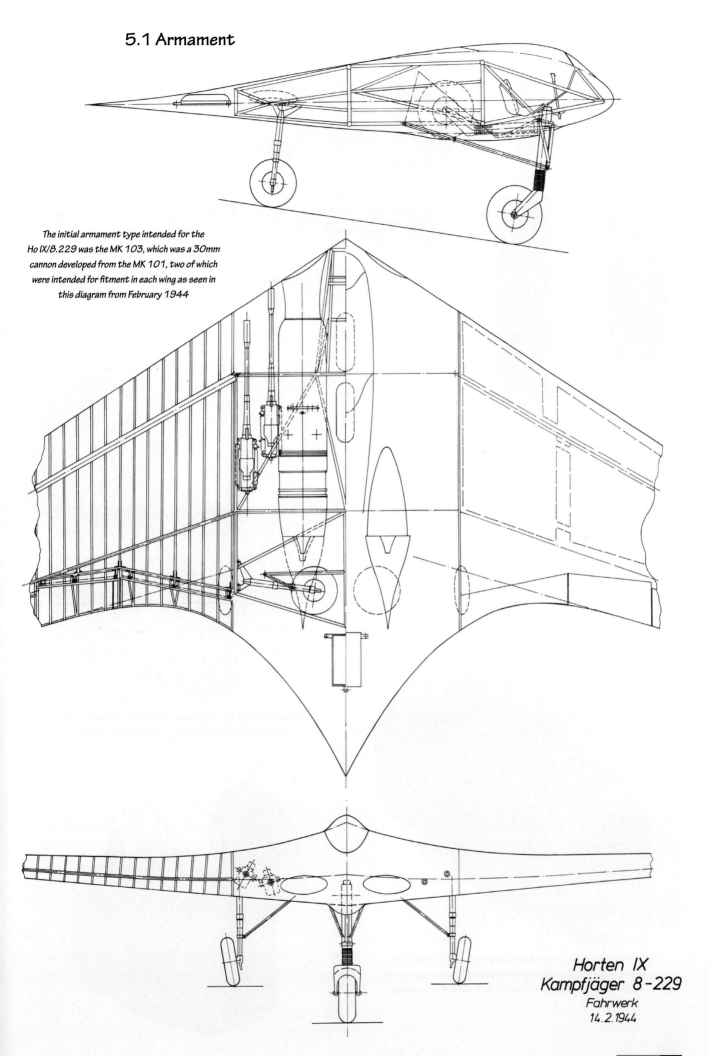

The initial armament type intended for the Ho IX/8.229 was the MK 103, which was a 30mm cannon developed from the MK 101, two of which were intended for fitment in each wing as seen in this diagram from February 1944

Horten IX
Kampfjäger 8-229
Fahrwerk
14.2.1944

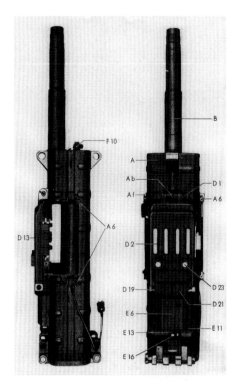

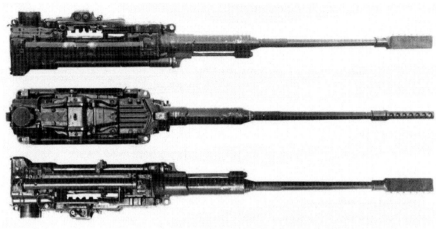

This set of three views of an MK 103 clearly shows the type's overall shape and its long barrel with muzzle brake

The other cannon type intended for the Ho IX/8.229 was the MK 108, which was a lightened development of the MK 103 with a shorter barrel and blow-back operating system. Its more compact physical nature meant it was more adaptable and thus saw more service use than the MK 103

5.2 Sighting

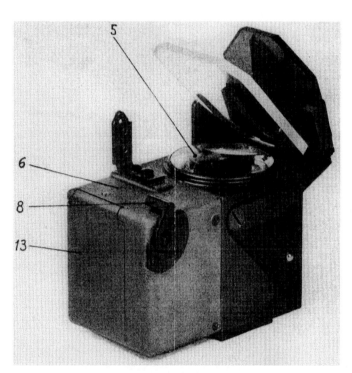

The initial sight intended for the Ho IX/8.229 was the Revi 16B, as shown in these two images from the type's manual

The Ho IX/8.229 was going to adopt the gyroscopic EZ42 gunsight, as seen here, but the sight was only ever produced in very small amounts and was never widely adopted by the Luftwaffe before the war ended

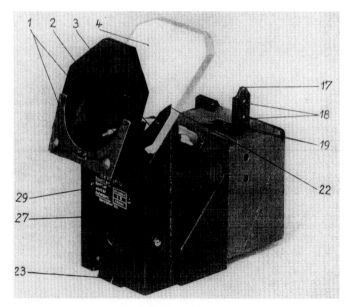

5.3 Radio

The Ho IX was initially fitted with the FuG 16ZY radio, as seen here in the remote form in the back of the Fw 190F-8 owned by NASM (©Scott Willey)

It is possible that the Ho 229 would have used a 'Morane mast' for the FuG radio installation, this mast was usually fitted via a wooden insulating block with a metal surround under the port wing, as seen here on a Bf 109G-6

Note: The FuG 16 was replaced by the FuG 15 with the V2 and would therefore have been adopted by the Ho 229 had it ever reached production – sadly we have found no illustration of this radio type

The production Ho 229 would most likely have carried a D/F loop, as seen here underneath NASM's Fw 190F-8; on the Ho 229 it would most likely have been situated on the dorsal spine aft of the cockpit and between the engines (©Scott Willey)

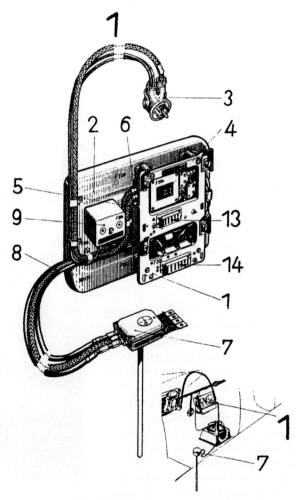

The production Ho 229 would have used the FuG 25A IFF, the installation of this is illustrated here from the Fw 190 manual

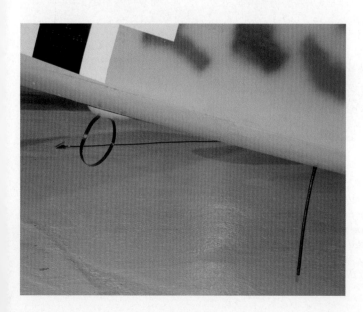

This shot of the Fw 190 currently on display at Cosford clearly shows the DF loop ahead of the whip antenna for the FuG 25a IFF – the latter aerial on the Ho 229 would have most likely have been under the centre section, aft of the wheel well

The Ho IX V1 centre-section outside the garage in which it was built prior to movement to the airfield for final assembly. You can clearly see the soft demarcation between upper and lower colours

Section 2

Camouflage & Markings

As always, I will start by saying that nothing is certain when trying to determine colours from old black and white photographs, and this combined with that fact that the Ho 229 never reached series production or operational use by the Luftwaffe means that you have a very limited amount of period visual images on which to base any study of colour and markings. Most, if not all, of the 'operational' schemes are highly subjective and some may be works of pure fantasy, but they are included to illustrate the schemes the type may have adopted had it reached operational service with the Luftwaffe in the latter stages of WWII. Just remember, nothing is an absolute when it comes to camouflage and markings, and that especially applies to late war Luftwaffe!

Although we all use the term 'RLM' to prefix Luftwaffe colours it should be noted that in period documents the only colour designated in

This shot clearly shows the glossy finish of the Ho IX V1

this manner was RLM 02, the rest were simply prefixed 'Farbton' (shade/tone/hue of a colour). The confusion lies in the fact that the main paint manufacturer (Warnecke und Böhm) issued paint charts that prefixed all colours with 'RLM', followed by Farbton 70, 71, 72 etc. However for consistency throughout this book we will prefix all colours with 'RLM'.

Prototypes

Reimar Horten said that he never really considered any scheme for the Ho IX, instead they 'just used paints that were readily available'. No RLM official painting diagram was ever created for the production Ho 229 either.

Horten IX V1

This machine was most likely a dark green (RLM 71) over light blue (RLM 65) and the whole airframe was then sealed with a glossy shellac (varnish). The two colours were applied with an airbrush, so the demarcation along each side of the nose (inside each wing root) and along the leading edge of the wings was soft-edged. Type B3 crosses were placed above the wings, positioned at midway along the ailerons and pointing directly forward, not following the angle of the wing leading edge. The images of it on its nose at two different times confirms that the same style and location of cross was also applied underneath each wing. A walkway region, framed by a thin red line, was applied on the upper surface of the inboard centre section (at the outer wing panel joint) and at some stage 'Hier Betreten!' (literally, enter here! – but basically means walk here only) was applied in red (or black) at the trailing edge of the port side of the centre-section, inboard of the walkway region (as two lines of text, with 'Hier' above 'Betreten'). Note that the walkway line went around the forward and aft spar access panels (oblong for the front and half-circle for the aft) and inboard of the *Hier Betreten* stencil was a data panel, with all the type's weights etc., which placed it basically alongside the braking parachute box. No other stencils (including tyre pressure marks on the wheel spats) can be seen on any period images.

Horten IX V2

This airframe was most likely in the same RLM 71 over 65 scheme as the V1 and again the demarcation between each colour is soft-edged. The crosses applied above and below the wings are Type B3 but sadly there are insufficient existing period images of sufficient clarity to identify any other markings or stencils. The addition of engines means that the walkway seen on the V1 would not be possible and the clarity of surviving images is not sufficient to identify if things like tyre pressure stencils were applied to the undercarriage doors. The only thing you can see is that the intake surrounds look to be unpainted metal.

This shot of the top of the Ho IX V1 clearly shows the dark upper surface, its glossy finish and the walkway marking, Heir Betreten stencil and the airframe data panel inboard of it

The Ho IX V2 nearing completion in a three-car garage, this shot allows you to see how the ply panels cover the wings and centre-section. This would later have needed some form of primer coat before the final camouflage paint was applied

The Ho IX V2 at Oranienburg with Lt Erwin Ziller starting an engine, the quality is not sufficient on this or any other image to determine the scheme and markings. You can however see the bare metal surrounds to the engine intakes

Ho 229 V3

Regardless of what some sources state, period images show that this airframe never had any paint applied by Gotha, other than protective paint on the metal regions, so any artwork created showing it in full markings (usually with Type B5 or B6 crosses) are works of pure speculation. The scheme therefore seen on this airframe within NASM's collection today is that which was applied during the 'renovation to display condition' undertaken at Freeman Field, Indiana in 1946 and it is most likely that all the colours applied were of American manufacturer (close approximations to the blues and greys seen on late-war Luftwaffe types). It is also likely that the airframe was painted in a scheme and colours representative of other Luftwaffe types captured post-war by US forces and moved to the USA for evaluation, as the centre section and wings were from different locations, so although it may seem possible they were painted and marked, by that stage in the war it is highly unlikely. This is probably why it currently looks to be in a scheme of RLM 76 underneath and RLM 74/75 on top. When the airframe underwent remedial conservation work in 2012/2019 it was found that the area under the metal exhaust shrouds was green, again this may be paint that originated in the USA, or it may be genuine paint

(RLM 02?) applied when the shrouds were originally installed by Gotha (personally, it looks a bit too bright green for RLM 02 to me, it's more like faded US Interior Green?). None of the markings applied are the correct

proportions, size or location, with the huge swastikas being in vogue in the immediate post-war period, as you will see them on other ex-Luftwaffe types displayed in the USA in the late 1940s.

The Ho IX V3 on capture, this rear view allows you to see the metal covers over the engines and the shrouds aft of them (these must be primed, as otherwise they would be more mottled in appearance). The dark areas are ply and you can see what looks to be tape (straight lines) and filler (blobs) used to seal the joints and fill the nail and screw heads etc.

The Ho IX V3 on arrival at Freeman Field in the USA, you can see it remained much as found when captured, but Horten employees finished such things as the missing port leading edge intake, plus various covers and access panels on the upper decking area. What colours the metal undercarriage doors were is anyone's guess [primer?] (©USAF)

The Ho IX V3 assembled with its wings in the Douglas factory in Chicago, by this stage it had received a paint scheme at Freeman Field, along with spurious markings including those huge swastikas!

(via Internet)

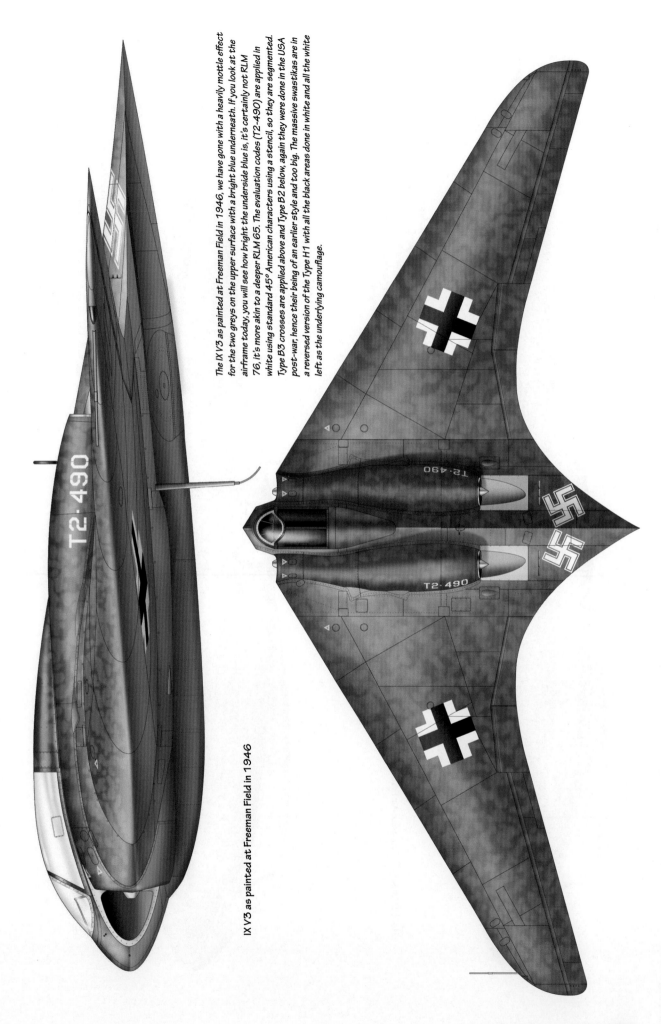

The IX V3 as painted at Freeman Field in 1946, we have gone with a heavily mottle effect for the two greys on the upper surface with a bright blue underneath. If you look at the airframe today, you will see how bright the underside blue is, it's certainly not RLM 76, it's more akin to a deeper RLM 65. The evaluation codes (T2-490) are applied in white using standard 45° American characters using a stencil, so they are segmented. Type B3 crosses are applied above and Type B2 below, again they were done in the USA post-war, hence their being of an earlier style and too big. The massive swastikas are in a reversed version of the Type H1 with all the black areas done in white and all the white left as the underlying camouflage.

IX V3 as painted at Freeman Field in 1946

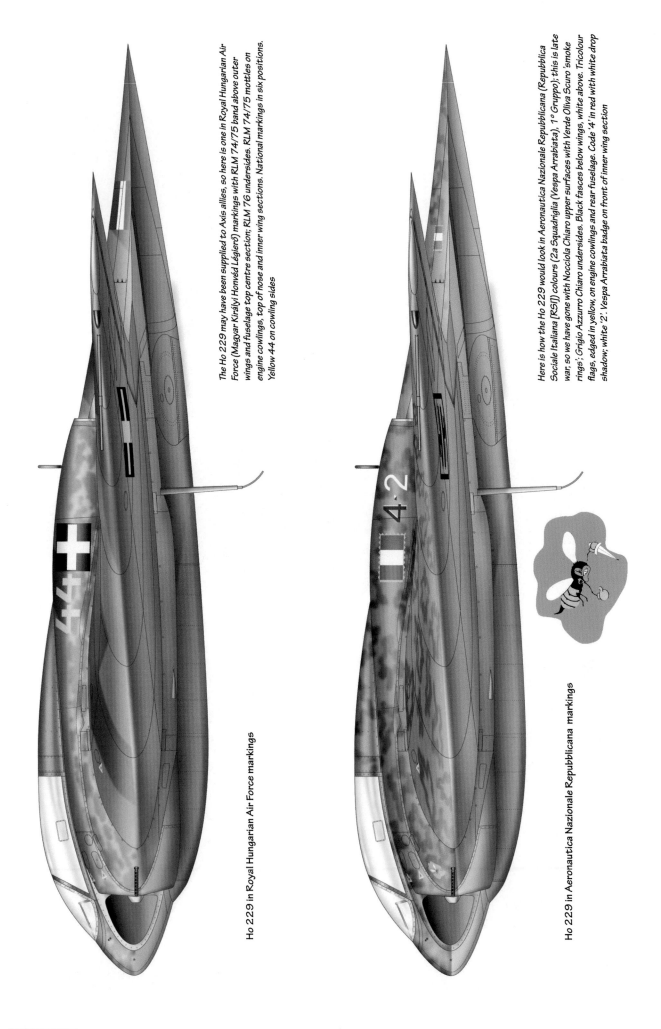

The Ho 229 may have been supplied to Axis allies, so here is one in Royal Hungarian Air Force (Magyar Királyi Honvéd Légierő) markings with RLM 74/75 band above outer wings and fuselage top centre section; RLM 76 undersides. RLM 74/75 mottles on engine cowlings, top of nose and inner wing sections. National markings in six positions. Yellow 44 on cowling sides

Ho 229 in Royal Hungarian Air Force markings

Here is how the Ho 229 would look in Aeronautica Nazionale Repubblicana (Repubblica Sociale Italiana [RSI]) colours (2a Squadriglia (Vespa Arrabiata), 1° Gruppo); this is late war, so we have gone with Nocciola Chiaro upper surfaces with Verde Oliva Scuro 'smoke rings'; Grigio Azzurro Chiaro undersides. Black fasces below wings, white above. Tricolour flags, edged in yellow, on engine cowlings and rear fuselage. Code '4' in red with white drop shadow; white '2'. Vespa Arrabiata badge on front of inner wing section

Ho 229 in Aeronautica Nazionale Repubblicana markings

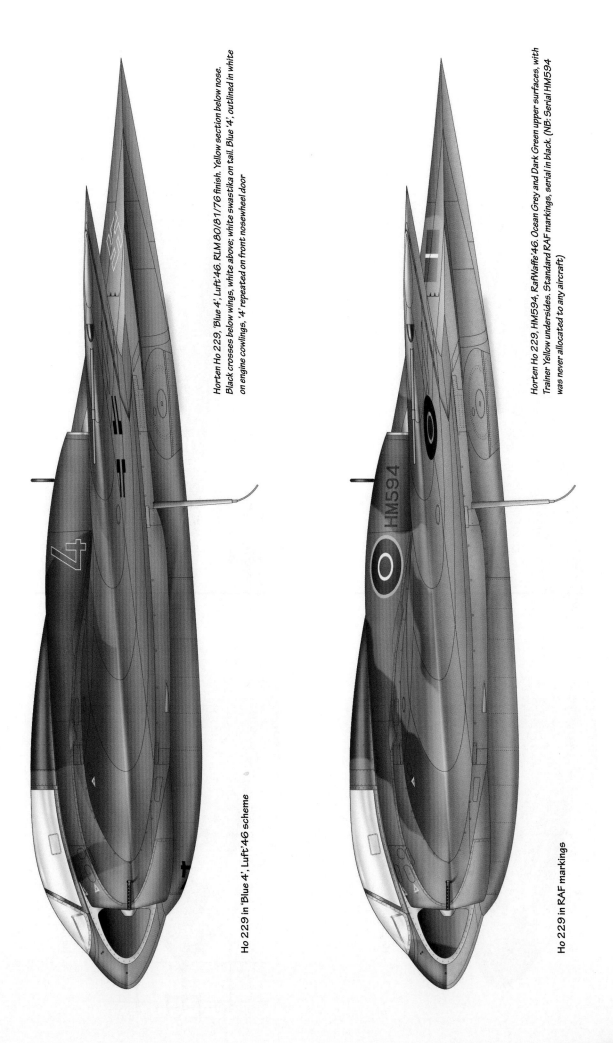

Horten Ho 229, 'Blue 4', Luft '46. RLM 80/81/76 finish. Yellow section below nose. Black crosses below wings, white above; white swastika on tail. Blue '4', outlined in white on engine cowlings, '4' repeated on front nosewheel door

Ho 229 in 'Blue 4', Luft '46 scheme

Horten Ho 229, HM594, RafWaffe '46. Ocean Grey and Dark Green upper surfaces, with Trainer Yellow undersides. Standard RAF markings, serial in black. (NB: Serial HM594 was never allocated to any aircraft)

Ho 229 in RAF markings

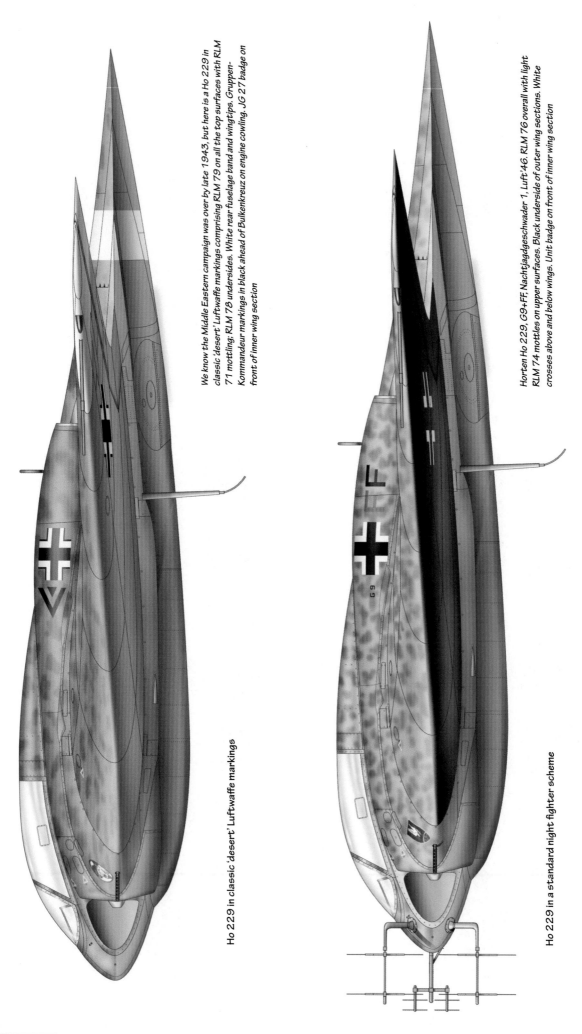

We know the Middle Eastern campaign was over by late 1943, but here is a Ho 229 in classic 'desert' Luftwaffe markings comprising RLM 79 on all the top surfaces with RLM 71 mottling. RLM 78 undersides. White rear fuselage band and wingtips. Gruppen-Kommandeur markings in black ahead of Bulkenkreuz on engine cowling. JG 27 badge on front of inner wing section

Ho 229 in classic 'desert' Luftwaffe markings

Horten Ho 229, G9+FF, Nachtjagdgeschwader 1, Luft '46. RLM 76 overall with light RLM 74 mottles on upper surfaces. Black underside of outer wing sections. White crosses above and below wings. Unit badge on front of inner wing section

Ho 229 in a standard night fighter scheme

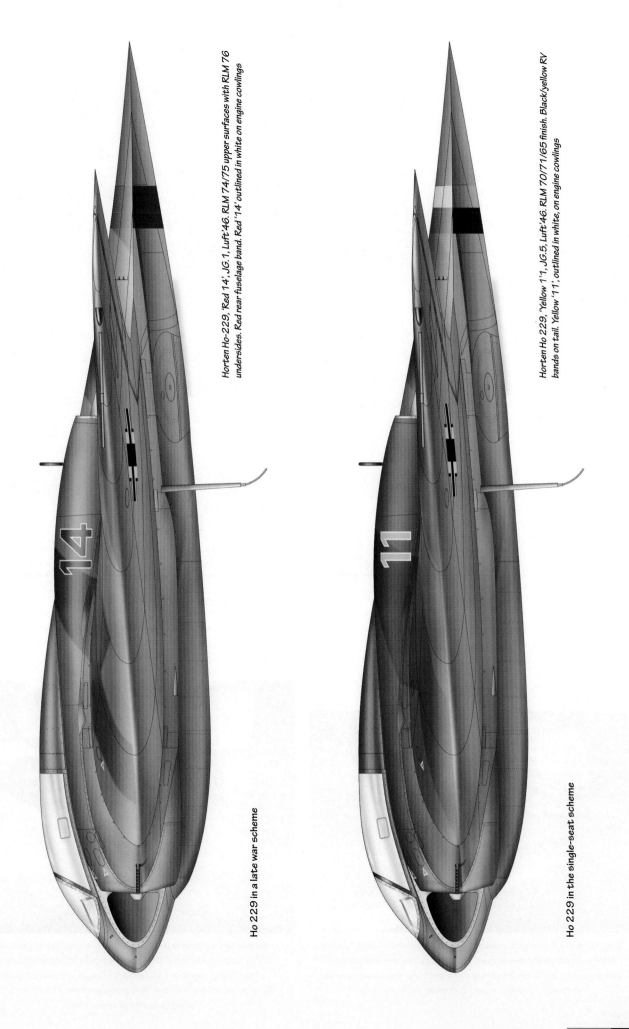

Horten Ho-229, 'Red 14', JG.1, Luft'46. RLM 74/75 upper surfaces with RLM 76 undersides. Red rear fuselage band. Red '14' outlined in white on engine cowlings

Ho 229 in a late war scheme

Horten Ho 229, 'Yellow 11', JG.5, Luft'46. RLM 70/71/65 finish. Black/yellow RV bands on tail. Yellow '11', outlined in white, on engine cowlings

Ho 229 in the single-seat scheme

Ho 229 V4, V5 & V6

None of these were ever fully completed and although the V6 had the engines etc. installed when captured, none of the outer skins were attached and the wings would have been manufactured elsewhere, so nothing was painted.

A & B-series (projected)

Neither the A or B series were ever put into production, so again any claims regarding their camouflage and markings are pure speculation. Most seem to go for the RLM 81/82 (or 82/83) over 76 scheme for the single-seat A-series, while the two-seat B-series is shown in a variety of schemes, most based on late-war Luftwaffe night-fighters and tend to therefore be RLM 76 overall with mottle or squiggles of RLM 75 on the upper surfaces.

What we have decided to offer on pages 52 to 55 though is a series of 'what if?' schemes, not really to show how it might have looked, as the Ho 229 is unlikely to have ever reached squadron use, regardless of plans, and even had it done so it would have been highly modified, but to show the type in some well known schemes, just so you can see what it looks like in classic WWII Axis (and captured) colours.

We would also recommend the following titles for those wishing to read more on the complex subject of Luftwaffe camouflage and markings:
• Luftwaffe Camouflage & Markings 1933-1945 Volume Two by K.A. Merrick & J. Kiroff (Classic Publications 2005 ISBN: 1-903223-39-3)
• Luftwaffe Colours 1935-1945 by Michael Ullmann (Hikoki Publications 2002 & 2008 ISBN: 978-1-9021090-7-7)
• The Official Monogram Painting Guide to German Aircraft 1935-1935 by K.A. Merrick & T.H. Hitchcock (Monogram Aviation Publications 1980 ISBN: 0-914144-29-4)

This is all of the Ho IX V6 that was captured by US forces at Friedrichroda in April 1945; as you can see the framework was primed, probably in something like RLM 02? (©US Army)

The Ho IX V4 was a little more complete on capture, but as you can see not much. The framework is primed and the metal panels around the engines look to be one consistent tone, so they too are probably primed (bare steel or aluminium tend to have a mottled look, even in black & white images). The wooden structure looks to be un-primed (©US Army)

While the Ho IX V3 underwent remedial conservation work in 2012-2019 some of the underside panels were removed, and as you can see they were painted a dark grey colour, but this may have been applied post-war when the airframe was 'restored for display purposes' at Freeman Field (©Scott Willey)

Also discovered whilst the Ho IX V3 underwent remedial conservation work in 2012-2019 was this area of green paint under the metal shrouds aft of each engine – again this may actually be a post-war American paint. The main colours were also most likely applied post-war in the USA, the huge swastikas certainly were! (©NASM)

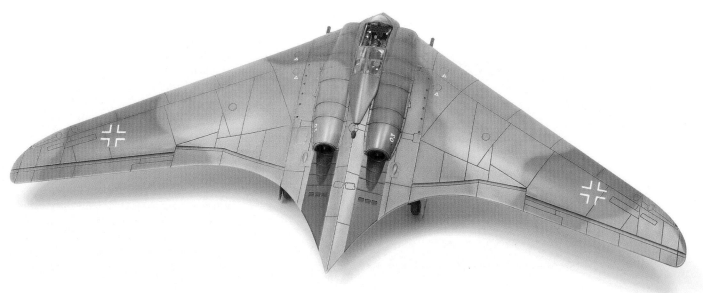

Section 3

Small Scale Horten

A fascination by model manufacturers with the flying wings of the Horten brothers meant that they were popular long before things like 'Luftwaffe 46' or 'what if?' came into vogue, probably supported by the fact that these aircraft were not pure fantasy and most of them actually flew, including the Ho IX prototype. The old and basic kit from PM (initially released under the Pioneer 2 label) and the pretty good kit from Revell in 1/72nd scale plus the DML/Dragon ones in 1/48th, were recently joined by those in 1/32nd and 1/48th from Zoukei-Mura. The latter company eventually further used the information it had gathered on those larger scale kits so it could enter, for the first time, the 1/72nd and 1/144th scale markets.

Zoukei-Mura 1/72nd
Horten Ho 229

by Libor Jekl

The main feature of this manufacturer, seen in their larger scale kits, is the fact that they are highly detailed, not just offering the traditional sub-assemblies for the cockpit or wheel bays, but all the airframe internal structure, engines, armament, fuel system and/or other major sections. This latest small-scale version is no different and it comes in a rather large rigid box featuring some nice 'what if?' style artwork on the top. The box contains twelve sprues

moulded in light grey-coloured plastic plus two clear ones, all separately and carefully packed and marked with regard to the two kits provided - 1/72nd and 1/144th. The moulding quality is on a high level as can be seen with things like the single-piece front fairing of the fuselage nacelle. However, on closer inspection there is some flash visible and rather thick sprue attachments on the inner tubular structures that will require a lot of cleaning up if you intend building the

All model photos ©Libor Jekl 2020

This shot clearly shows the complex and rather fragile main framework assembly

Technical Specifications

Manufacturer: Zoukei-Mura, Japan

Scale: 1/144th & 1/72nd

Kit No.: SWS 1/144 & 1/72 No.1

Materials: Injection Moulded Plastic

The engines make up next and then fit into the framework

Viewed from the top and bottom, here are the engines in situ

kit with this all exposed. The inner structure forms an integral part of the airframe and cannot be left out because it contains the cockpit and landing gear, so very careful trimming and overall assembly work all needs to be approached with care and patience. The kit provides detailed inner wing and fuselage nacelle details, Jumo 004B-2 engines, 30mm MK 103 cannon along with their ammunition boxes, as well as a detailed cockpit and wheel bays. Obviously, some parts have been simplified in comparison with their larger scale kits; for instance, you don't have to assemble individual carriers for the rotor and stator compressor blades inside the engines. The surface of the various panels on the nacelle and wing halves features finely engraved panel lines, which are somewhat limited considering the wooden nature of the airframe skin. There are also subtly raised covers, filling and inspection ports along with screw and rivet lines on the metal parts of the nacelle. The canopy looks crystal clear and it is split into two parts, so it can be displayed open.

The components for the 1/144th scale kit are provided on a single sprue with a separate canopy, and do look more conventional. The base airframe is assembled via two main parts and despite these being rather thick, no sink marks or moulding defects are visible. The surface is highly detailed and there is a reasonably good overall look to the smaller parts; obviously some of them are simplified due to moulding limitations, but you get a full cockpit and open wheel bays. The instructions are not stylised into a booklet as seen with their larger scale kits, but are still very informative and provide the maximum amount of information needed for the build, including pointing out challenging parts of the assembly. They also include three-view diagrams helping to achieve the correct geometry, and close-up details of the internal structures required to get proper alignment. The painting guide refers to Vallejo Color and Gunze-Sangyo Mr Color ranges and the camouflage and markings section offers a spurious option for a machine in a Luftwaffe night fighter scheme (although the plane does not carry any radar equipment nor a gunsight) for the 1/72nd scale kit and a single day fighter scheme for the 1/144th kit. Surprisingly the large decal sheet contains, apart from national insignias, a set of Luftwaffe numerals in four colours, three styles of Reich Defence bands and a set of stencil data; the same is provided for the 1/144th version, so fans of alternative history can go to town.

Construction

Before the build actually starts, you have to first consider what configuration you want to depict, as this effects the construction sequence along with the painting of the individual sub-assemblies. My first intention was to build the kit in an unfinished condition as it was discovered by American troops in April 1945, which the kit basically allows with only a reasonable amount of extra work. I eventually gave way to the fantastic shape of the completed flying wing and decided to finish it, with a little imagination, in the form it would (potentially) have adopted during service trials.

The first step is the assembly the Jumo engines, each consisting of several parts, and they do look busy and well detailed once completed. However, if you want to make a fully exposed airframe, I suspect some extra details would further enhance the look and add more realism such as various wiring and piping lines. The basis of the fuselage nacelle forms the tubular frame in which the individual parts of the cockpit side framing and engine bearers are fixed. In this scale the construction is rather challenging and needs a careful and well thought out approach, since the frame construction itself is brittle and difficult to handle – there is all the time a real danger of breaking some part of it. Fortunately, the plastic used does

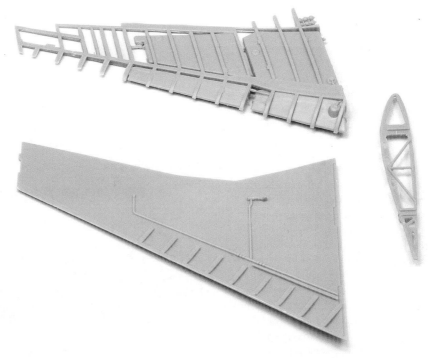

The wings include a lot of internal structure, including the fuel tanks, and it's best to include it all as it lends strength to the completed wings

With the centre section and wings completed, the nose and upper and lower centre-section skins make up the bulk of the model

intend to expose these, as it adds some rigidity to the assembled model. Now we are done with the main sub-assemblies, these can be trial fitted without using any glue; all should go together without using excessive force. At this stage it is necessary to paint all the visible sections such as the cockpit and wheel bay structures, although because the engines are barely visible through the wheel bays, I eventually left them alone in the base black primer colour. The structure was then primed

not seem to break that easily and it is quite flexible. In addition, the whole construction gets more unstable once you gradually add parts to it, which in turn makes it difficult to precisely fit the components to it. It is obvious that the accurate assembly of this frame structure is fundamental for keeping the correct geometry of the model at a later stage when the individual surface panels and wing halves will be fixed onto it. Its rigidity is improved only by the installation of the engine lower panels in the next step, after which the assembly and manipulation are a bit easier. Next the MK 103 cannon were assembled along with their ammunition boxes and wing ribs. Since I planned to finish the kit completely covered, I did not have to deal with the detail painting of these assemblies. Now the engines could be inserted into their bearers and secured via a couple of fixing pins, ensuring their correct position. The nacelle frame was then finished with the addition of its upper part, which is moulded as a single piece.

Onto wing assembly now, where I recommend you cement the inside of the complete inner structure comprising the spars and ribs along with the fuel cell even if you do not

The interior was left in its black primer for the main areas, only the cockpit interior was picked out in RLM 66. The engines would benefit from additional detail and painting, but only if you intend to have them exposed

with Mr Finishing Surfacer 1500 (Black) and the cockpit components were airbrushed RLM 66 (H416), while the undercarriage parts visible through the openings were done in RLM 02 (H70). To the seat I added belts that came from the Eduard etched set (#SS582 Seat Belts Luftwaffe WWII Fighters - Steel) and all the details such as the headrest, control boxes, control stick etc. were picked out in Vallejo acrylics. For the instrument panel and sidewall panel there is the alternative of using the decals supplied.

Next I joined the wing halves to the central nacelle frame and continued with the front single-piece fairing, although before this one went on I removed the cannon barrels so that they could be re-attached later. Then I carefully continued with the individual nacelle surface panels working from the top to the bottom. The overall assembly required some adjustment or trimming of parts of the inner tubular frame to get the parts fitting as closely as possible. I still needed to address some gaps with white Milliput around the main wing joints, though. Again, I can only highlight the need for very careful assembly and lining up all frame parts properly at the earlier assembly stages. The joints were then sanded smooth, cleaned up and damaged panel lines restored. The final tasks were to attach the engine top cowls and the windshield.

Camouflage & Markings

The kit received a primer layer of Mr Surfacer 1000 (Grey) and all surface blemishes that had appeared were sorted out, and the surface was then polished with fine grades of Mr Finishing Cloths. While browsing the references for a hypothetical camouflage scheme I eventually decided to follow the appearance of another late-war Luftwaffe prototype instead. Therefore, I ignored the night fighter scheme offered in the kit and went for a fighter scheme consisting of RLM 81 (H421) and RLM 82 (H422) on the upper surfaces with RLM 76 (H417) underneath, which the V3 prototype could theoretically have worn after its completion. The area behind the engine's exhaust would, in my opinion, be treated with a heat resistant black paint used on the fuselage sides of things like the Bf 109 or Fw 190, so the exposed area was masked off and sprayed with black (H12). From my decal bank I added a fictional prototype designation code and placed it on either side of the engines, while from the kit's decal sheet I used only the crosses and the fuel data stencilling. The decals are printed thinly with sharp register and they worked really nicely.

Final Details

The front undercarriage leg is moulded in two halves, split vertically, which is a little unusual, so you need to carefully clean the visible joint line. Thankfully this leg could be

The wings are now added to the centre-section framework

Fitting the outer skins to the centre-section is one of the more complex aspects of this kit because they don't fit well, as proven by the amount of filler needed around the wing roots

The model is primed with Mr Surfacer 1000 and this highlights any areas that need additional attention, as well as where panels lines removed by sanding will need to be re-established

Always start painting with the lightest colour, in this instance RLM 76 for the undersides, with shading done using a slightly darkened version

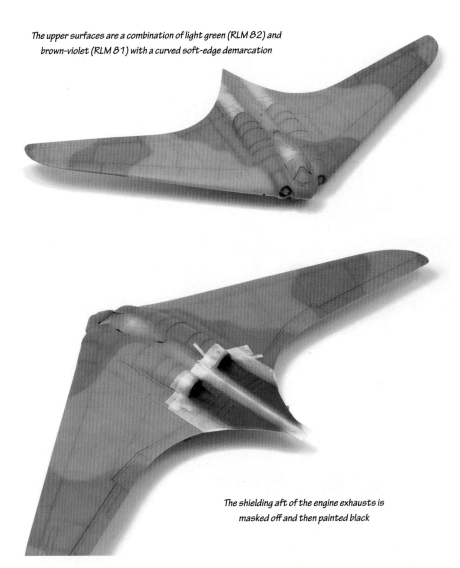

The upper surfaces are a combination of light green (RLM 82) and brown-violet (RLM 81) with a curved soft-edge demarcation

The shielding aft of the engine exhausts is masked off and then painted black

assembled without inserting the wheel in it, which could instead be installed after painting the parts because the plastic is flexible enough to withstand bending of the wheel pins. Fixing the legs and their struts in the bays was an easy task thanks to their precise fit and clearly defined openings for them. The correct sit of the model could be then checked against three-view drawings in the instructions that even quote all the main angles. The DF loop antenna was replaced with a new item cut and bent from copper wire and the 'Morane mast' antenna was thinned on a sanding stick to look more appropriate. Eventually, I inserted into the wing the separated gun barrels and fixed the rear part of canopy in the open position using a small piece of Blu Tack attached under the overpainted portion of the canopy, that thus avoided using cyanoacrylate and the possible risk of spilling it onto the model's surface.

Verdict

The entry of Zoukei-Mura into the 1/72nd scale market is very welcome news and this hopefully won't be a single example and they will soon follow up with other types from their portfolio, such as the Skyraider, Ki-45 or Hs 129, because done to this level would definitely be very tempting in this scale. On the other hand, the concept of Zoukei-Mura kits is not intended for the broader spectrum of model hobbyists due to their rather challenging construction requiring a high degree of skill. It is squarely aimed at a specific group of model-makers that admire highly detailed kits that can be built straight from the box without further investments in the aftermarket.

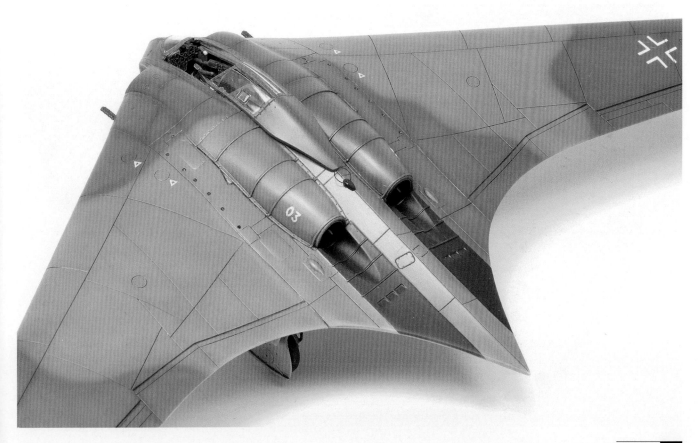

Once glossed and the markings applied the final detail parts are the undercarriage, seen here in its component form plus the rear section of the canopy, which in this instance would be held in place with Blu Tack

Paints used

Gunze-Sangyo Mr Aqueous Color:
- H12 Black
- H70 RLM 02 Grau
- H416 RLM 66 Schwarzgrau
- H417 RLM 76 Hellblau
- H421 RLM 81 Braunviolet
- H422 RLM 82 Hellgrün
- Mr Surfacer 1000 (Grey)
- Mr Finishing Surfacer 1500 (Black)

Small Scale Horten

Built size comparison

Horten IX/Ho 229 Kits

The lists below are as comprehensive as possible, but if there are amendments or additions, please contact the author via the Valiant Wings Publishing address shown at the front of this title.

All kits are injection moulded plastic unless otherwise stated.

1/144th

- Brengun Horten Ho 229A #BRP144007 (2018) – New tooling
- Brengun Horten Ho 229 Night Fighter #BRS144010 (2018)
- Zoukei-Mura Horten Ho 229A #TBA – *Originally announced for 2018, released in 2019 combined with 1/72nd kit (see 1/72nd scale list)*

1/72nd

- Airmodel [vac] Go 229 V1 #AM-019 (1969-1980)
- Airmodel [vac] Gotha Go 229A01 (Ho IX V3) #AM-126 (1972) – *Under Frank Modellbau ownership*
- A+V Models [res/mtl/pe/vac] Horten Ho 229 V1 #AV 061 (1997)
- Boleslav [vac] Go 229 V3 #N/K (early 1980s) – *One-man operation, only a few produced*
- Combat Models (ex-Airmodel) [vac] Gotha Go 229 #72-0101 (1984-2004)
- Dragon Ho 229 Flying Wing 'with Interior' #5027 – *Announced 2005, not released to date*
- Dragon Model & Pattern Works [res] Gotha (Horten) Ho 229 #N/K (1986) – *Firm changed its name to Fisher Model & Pattern in the mid-1990s*
- Intermodel (ex-Airmodel) [vac] Go 229A01 Ho IX V3 #IU-11 (early 70s) – *Probably the Go 229 V1 kit*
- Jasmine Model [pe] Ho 229 'Fill Structure PE Detail Model' #202002 (2013)
- JK Resin Models [res] Gotha/Horten Ho.IX #N/K (1996->)

- JRC {Japan Resin Craft} [res] Gotha Go 229A-01 #N/K (early 80s)
- Matchbox (ex-PM) Ho 229A-1 #40147 (1995)
- MikroMir Horten Ho IX V1 #TBA – *Announced for 2020*
- Pioneer 2 (ex-PM Model) Horten Ho 229A-1 (Ho IX) #4005 (1987)
- PM Model Horten Ho 229A-1 #PM-210 – *Initially tooled as PMS, then did toolings for Pioneer 2 in UK (1982-1992), then started to release these toolings under the PM label – Brand was relaunched under new ownership in 2017*
- PM Model Horten 229 V7 'Nachtjäger' #PM-220 (1997)
- PMP a Escala [res] Horten Ho IX B-0 'Jumo 004B 04/1945' #AS72124 (2015)
- PMP a Escala [res] Horten Ho IX B-0 'Jumo 004D 05/1945' #AS72125 (2015)
- PSC 72 [vac] (ex-Boleslav) Go 229 #N/K (1984-89) – *Produced by a modelling group, also used the VTD logo*
- Revell Horten IX/Go 229 #04329 (1994) *New tooling* – Reissued in 2006 as Horten Go 229 (#04312)
- Sharkit [res] Horton IX 'Early Design' #N/K (2005) – *Release not confirmed*
- Zoukei-Mura Horten Ho 229A #TBA – *Originally announced for 2018, released in 2019 combined with 1/144th kit (see below)*
- Zoukei-Mura Horten Ho 229A #SWS 1/72 & 1/144 No.1 (2019) – *Combined 1/144th & 1/72nd scale kits*

1/48th

- Airmodel [vac] Gotha Go 229A-1 #AM-050 (1969-1980)
- Airmodel [vf] Gotha Go 229A-1 #AM-4801 (1969-2000) – *Under Frank Modellbau ownership after 1980*
- Blue Max – *See Schmidt Vacu-Modellbau*
- Dragon Horten Ho 229A-1 Flying Wing #5505 (1992) – *This was originally a Trimaster/Right Staff project and Dragon acquired the kit designs, neither firm ever officially announced it though prior to their demise – Reissued 2010 and 2016*

Notes

3DP	– 3D Printed
inj	– Injection Moulded Plastic
ltd inj	– Limited-run Injection Moulded Plastic
ma	– Self-adhesive tape masks
mtl	– White-metal (including Pewter)
pe	– Photo-etched metal
res	– Resin
vac	– Vacuum-formed Plastic
vma	– Vinyl self-adhesive paint masks
(1999)	– Denotes date the kit was released
(1994->)	– Date/s denote start/finish of firm's activities, the exact date of release of this kit is however unknown
ex-	– Denotes the tooling originated with another firm, the original tool maker is noted after the '-'

- Dragon Horten Ho 229B Nachtjäger #5511 (1993) – Reissued, same kit number, as Gotha Go 229 V6 Nightfighter in 2003
- Dragon-Shanghai Horten Ho 229A-1 Flying Wing #5505SH (2000)
- Hasegawa (ex-Dragon) Horten Ho 229A-1 #HD25 (1999)
- Hasegawa (ex-Dragon) Horten Ho 229B Nacht Jäger #HD11 (1994)
- Premiere Horten (Go 229) IX #3109 – *Announced 1990, then again for June 1992 but never released*
- Schmidt Vacu-Modellbau [vac] Gotha (Horten) Go 229 #4808 (1984-2000) – *Issued under their Blue Max label*
- Zoukei-Mura Horten Ho 229 #SWS48 No.3 (2015)

1/32nd

- Battledec (Clarke/Carpenter Associates) [vac] Gotha Go 229 #N/K (1966)
- Blue Max – *See Schmidt Vacu-Modellbau*
- Combat Models (ex-Schmidt Vacu-modellbau) [vac] Go-229 Horten #32-018 (1984-1997)
- Schmidt Vacu-Modellbau [vac] Gotha (Horten) Go 229 #3213 (1984-2000) – *Issued under their Blue Max label*
- Zoukei-Mura Horten Ho 229 #SWS 8 (2014)
- Zoukei-Mura Horten Ho 229B #TBA – *Announced for 2018, not released to date (a conversion set [SWS08-M05] should have been released by the time these words are read, so this kit may not be produced)*

Combat Models 32-018 built by owner (J Rucks)

Dragon 5505

Dragon 5511

Dragon 5505 built by author on release in 1992

Revell 04329 built by author on release in 1994

Pioneer 2 Ho 229 (4005)

Zoukei-Mura SWS 1-48 No 3

Zoukei-Mura SWS 72 and 144 No 1

Zoukei-Mura SWS No 8

Zoukei-Mura SWS 1-48 No 3 contents

Zoukei-Mura SWS No 8 press info

Appendix ii

Horten IX/Ho 229 Accessories/Masks

1/144th

• Brengun [pe] Ho 229A Detail Set #BRL144143 {Brengun}

1/72nd

• Airwaves [pe] Horten 229 Detail Set #AEC72150 {Revell}
• Equipage [res/rb] Gotha Go 229/Horten IX Wheel Set #72082
• Eduard [ma] Horten IX/Go 229 Canopy & Wheel Masks #CX179 {Revell}
• Eduard [pe] Horten IX/Go 229 Detail Set #72186 {Revell}
• Falcon [vac] Clear-Vax Set No.5 – *Includes canopy for PM single-seat kit*
• Pmask [vma] Horten Go 229 Canopy & Wheel Masks #Pk72112 {Revell}
• Rechlin Details [res] Gotha Ho 229 Control Surfaces #None {Revell}
• Squadron [vac] Horten Ho 229 Canopy #9121 {PM} – *Included 2x canopies for the PM single-seat kit*

1/48th

• Cutting Edge Modelworks [vma] Go 229 Canopy & Wheel Masks #CEBM48233 {Dragon}
• E-Z Masks [vma] Ho 229 Canopy & Wheel Masks #247 {Dragon}
• Falcon [vac] Clear-Vax Set No.16 – *Includes canopy for Dragon single-seat kit*
• Reheat Models [pe] Ho 229A-1 & B Detail Set #RH077 {Dragon}
• Scale Aircraft Conversions [wm] Ho 229 Undercarriage Set #48299 {Zoukei-Mura}

• Zoukei-Mura [res] Ho 229 Flight Sortie Preparation Set #SWS08-F04 {Zoukei-Mura}
• Zoukei-Mura [pe] Ho 229 Interior & Air Brake Detail Set #SWS48-03-M04 {Zoukei-Mura}
• Zoukei-Mura [res] Ho 229 Pilot Figure #SWS48-03-F01 {Zoukei-Mura}
• Zoukei-Mura [br] Ho 229 Turned Metal Machine Gun Barrels & Pitot Tube #SWS48-03-M03 {Zoukei-Mura}
• Zoukei-Mura [wm] Ho 229 Undercarriage Struts #SWS48-03-M01 {Zoukei-Mura}
• Zoukei-Mura [res] Ho 229 Weighted Tyres #SWS48-03-M02 {Zoukei-Mura}
• Zoukei-Mura [pe] Ho 229 Wood Grain Masks, Type 1 #SWS48-03-M06 {Zoukei-Mura}
• Zoukei-Mura [pe] Ho 229 Wood Grain Masks, Type 2 #SWS48-03-M07 {Zoukei-Mura}

1/32nd

• G Factor [br] Ho 229 Landing Gear #32038 {Zoukei-Mura}
• HGW Models [pa/pe] Ho 229 Orlon Seat Belt Set #132557 {Zoukei-Mura}
• Yahu Models [pe] Ho 229 Instrument Panel #YMA3255 {Zoukei-Mura}
• Zoukei-Mura [pe] Ho 229 Interior & Air Brake Detail Set #SWS08-M04 {Zoukei-Mura}
• Zoukei-Mura [res] Ho 229 Combustion Chamber #SWS08-M06 {Zoukei-Mura}
• Zoukei-Mura [res] Ho 229 Ground Crew Set #SWS08-F02 {Zoukei-Mura}
• Zoukei-Mura [res] Ho 229 Flight Assistant Set #SWS08-F03 {Zoukei-Mura}
• Zoukei-Mura [res] Ho 229 Pilot Figure #SWS08-F01 {Zoukei-Mura}
• Zoukei-Mura [wm] Ho 229 Undercarriage Legs #SWS08-M01 {Zoukei-Mura}
• Zoukei-Mura [res] Ho 229 Weighted Tyres #SWS08-M02 {Zoukei-Mura}

Reheat Models RH077   Scale Aircraft Conversions 48299

• Zoukei-Mura [br] Ho 229 Turned Metal Machine Gun and Pitot Tube Set #SWS08-M03 {Zoukei-Mura}
• Zoukei-Mura [pe] Ho 229 Wood Grain Masks, Type 1 #D29325 {Zoukei-Mura}
• Zoukei-Mura [pe] Ho 229 Wood Grain Masks, Type 2 #D29332 {Zoukei-Mura}
• Zoukei-Mura [res] Ho 229 V7 2-seat Conversion Set #SWS08-M05 {Zoukei-Mura}

Decals

Note: To date there have been no decal sheets produced that offered any markings relating to the Ho IX or Ho 229, the only sheets thus far produced all relate to replicating the wood grain effect of its construction (see below)

1/48th – Uschi van der Rosten
#1023 Ho 229 Special Wood Grain Decal Set

1/32nd – Uschi van der Rosten
#1020 Ho 229 Special Wood Grain Decal Set

1/32nd – Zoukei-Mura
#SWS08-D01 Wood Grain Decal Set for Ho 229

The Ho IX V1 outside the garage in which it was built, its small overall size well illustrated by the Horten employee in the cockpit

 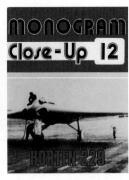 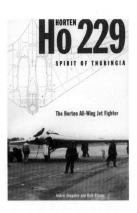  

Appendix iii

Bibliography

This list of Horten Ho IX/Ho 229 related publications is as comprehensive as possible, but there are bound to be omissions so if you have amendments or additions, please contact the author via the Valiant Wings Publishing address shown at the front of this title.

Official Documents

No official manuals were ever produced for the type, as it never entered series production or Luftwaffe service.

Publications

• Camouflage & Markings of the Luftwaffe Aircraft Vol.1 Day Fighters, Model Art Special No.308 (Model Art Co., Ltd)
• Cockpit Profile No.5 – Deutsche Flugzeugcockpits und Instrumentenbretter by P.W. Cohausz (Flugzeug Publikations GmbH)
• German Aircraft of the Second World War by J.R. Smith & A.L. Kay (Putnam, 1972)
• German Air Projects 1935-1945 Vol.2 – Fighters by M. Rys, Red Series No.5106 (Mushroom Model Publications 2004 ISBN: 83-89450-07-0)
• German Jets in WWI (Monogram Aviation Publications)
• German Jets in WWII, Model Art Special No.348 (Model Art Co., Ltd 1990)

• German Jets of World War Two by M. Griehl, Warbirds Illustrated No.52 (Arms & Armour Press 1988 ISBN: 1-85368-884-2)
• Horten Flying Wings in WWII by Dabrowski (Schiffer ISBN: 0-88740-357-3)
• Horten Ho 9 by D. Myhra: X-Planes of the Third Reich (Schiffer 2004 ISBN: 0-7643-0916-1)
• Horten Ho 9 by D. Myhra: X-Planes of the Third Reich (Schiffer ISBN: 0-7643-0916-1)
• Horten Ho 229 – Spirit of Thuringia by A. Shepelev & H. Ottens (Classic Publications 2007 ISBN: 1-903223-66-0)
• Horten Ho 229 by M. Murawski & M. Rys, Monogram Special Edition 3D (Kagero Publishing 2017 ISBN: 978-8365437-15-0)
• Horten Ho 229: Der Legendäre Nurflügel by A. Shepelev & H. Ottens (Motorbuch Verlag 2020 ISBN: 978-3613042-54-4)
• Luftwaffe Advanced Aircraft Projects to 1945, Vol.1 Fighters & Ground-Attack Aircraft; Arado to Junkers by Ingolf Meyer (Midland Publishing Ltd 2006 ISBN: 1-85780-240-3)
• Only the Wing by R.E. Lee (Smithsonian Institution Scholarly Press 2011, ISBN: 978-1935623-03-8)
• Operation Lusty: The Race for Hitler's Secret Technology by Graham M. Simons (Pen & Sword Books ©2016 ISBN: 978-147384-737-8)
• Secret German Aircraft Projects of 1945 (Toros Publications 1997) – *First published as 'Paper Planes of the Third Reich' by them in 1996*

• The Horten Brothers and their All-Wing Aircraft by D. Myhra (Schiffer Publishing Ltd 2004 ISBN: 0-7643-0441-0)
• The Horten Ho 9/Ho 229 Retrospective by D. Myhra (Schiffer Publishing Ltd ISBN: 0-7643-1666-4)
• The Horten Ho 9/Ho 229 Technical History by D. Myhra (Schiffer Publishing Ltd 2013 ISBN: 978-0763416-67-8)
• The Horten Flying Wings in World War II by H-P Dabrowski (Schiffer Publishing Ltd 1995 ISBN: 0-88740-886-9) – *Reprinted as The Horten Flying Wings of the Horten Brothers in 2004*
• The Warplanes of the Third Reich by William Green (Macdonald & Co Ltd, 1970)
• Unknown! No.5 by J. Miranda & P. Mercado (Reichdreams Research Services 2007)
• War Prizes: The Album by P. Butler (Midland Publishing 2006 ISBN: 1-85780-244-6)
• The Warplanes of the Third Reich by William Green (Macdonald & Co Ltd, 1970)

Periodicals & Part-works

• Air Pictorial April 1959
• Flying Review Vol.14 No.1
• RAF Flying Review, September 1958
• Scale Aircraft Modelling Vol.20 No.11 January 1999

The Ho IX V1 outside the hangar at Göttingen in March 1944, note the shadow of the photographer in the top left-hand